The Shepherd's Path

by

Georgia Frances Brister Morris

PITTSBURGH, PENNSYLVANIA 15222

ISBN: 978-1-4349-9679-4
Printed in the United States of America

First Printing

For more information or to order additional books, please contact:
RoseDog Books
701 Smithfield Street
Pittsburgh, Pennsylvania 15222
U.S.A.
1-800-834-1803
www.rosedogbookstore.com

DEDICATION

This chronicle of events is lovingly dedicated to the

memory of my parents, George Brister (1887-1985)

and Jessie Brister (1899 – 1996).

My father's code of living by example set:

"Any man who truly knows his life is right, that

His fellow men know that his word is better than gold,

Can walk with his head held high, his step firm, look any man

In the eye, and have no need to bow to anyone."

By

GEORGIA FRANCES BRISTER MORRIS

ACKNOWLEDGMENTS

This memoir records events in the life of the firstborn daughter of a Texas pioneer through many trails leading to the mountaintop. God had plans for this child.

Some 25 years ago, two friends at the First United Methodist Church of Dallas, Texas, Rev. Jim Reeves and his wife, Catherine, first advanced the idea that I should write this memoir. Catherine especially insisted that I do so. Family, friends, and business associates have offered encouragement and support. I am thankful for eight brothers and their families, my sister and her husband, Mary Evelyn and Bill R. Herman, my own family who have been the glue holding me together—George Edsel Morris and Molli-B Morris, and my grandchildren Tina Marie and Kayla Jean Morris and Andrew and Sarah Reiman. My great-grandchildren have not had the opportunity to know me, but it is hoped they will always cherish their heritage.

Without productive help from special people, this book may have remained scribbled notes and a tattered old scrapbook.

My niece, Kristi Rodriguez, struggled to convert notes and partially typed copy to the first manuscript. My stepson, Jerry Neill Morris, applied his computer knowledge to include in the book cherished photos, letters, and documents.

I want to thank my granddaughter, Sarah Reiman, for her artistic ability in transmitting my vision from idea to reality.

Most of all, I am grateful to Dr. Charles Emory Burton, the one professional who read the first manuscript, offered encouragement, and spent much time editing and researching sources for publication.

FOREWORD

Before the ravages of time complete the destruction of memories, this senior descendent of George and Jessie Brister feels compelled to record just a few highlights of this family's streak across the stage of history.

A great heritage has been bequeathed to our family and its preservation is imperative.

Because the personal journey of this writer has been touched by some special events in history, family, friends and associates pressed me to record a few.

My story could not be complete without my family. A few years ago a venture into this project produced a limited edition of a little book titled *From Rough Creek to the Potomac*. That was assigned to family and friends. A few incidents will be repeated in this version, because we hope it will appeal to a wider readership.

We hope to impart a sense of history, because the century we just lived through saw more changes than ever accomplished in any single century.

Perhaps we have moved beyond the mindset that prevailed about the time the steam engine was invented when Congress put forth a bill to close the patent office, because there simply could not be any more inventions.

From horse and buggy and sailboats, to the moon and back. Commerce and communication, science and medicine, transportation, refrigeration and the advent of technology leaves those of us over the age of 75 in a world of dot com, e-mail, automatic telephone systems of never ending menus to search for a knowledgeable human voice that never comes, seas of buttons to push we will never understand, yet we stand in awe of the wonders of the future and our young people who understand them, even as we worry that they cannot pick up pen and write a personal note or do a math equation without a calculator.

It will make us wish we could peer into the future and see what wonders await our great grandchildren.

Rather than regret what we cannot see or grieve for the unknown, we pray the world will become a better place where people can live in harmony, respecting one another's cultures, political systems and religions, knowing that one God, by whatever name, rules over us all and His will be done.

From the dawn of history, the human spirit has lived with the inborn instinct that longs for immortality and held visions of climbing that ladder into eternity...

It seems a complete mystery why there should be a conflict between the theories of evolution and intelligent design. No one knows when time began. In God's time each of the six days referred to in Genesis may have been six billion years in our calendar; thus allowing the evolution process to stand as a fact that should be accepted.
It is a process directed by the master Craftsman.

FAMILY TREE

Since the beginning of time, as we know it, man has striven to make life better for himself and his family.

So it was when a few acorns from the Brister, Powell, Huffstettler, Simmons and Fox families from Scotland, England, Germany, and Holland sailed the ocean blue in the early 1700s and settled in New England. Some branches then took root down in North Carolina.

Shortly after the treaties of 1805-1820 were signed with the Choctaw Indians, our forefathers joined the push to the West and settled in Mississippi and Arkansas.

Following the Civil War, Grandfather Brister returned from serving as a Confederate soldier and dreamed of a new beginning. He gathered his family, a few possessions and joined other families in a covered wagon train for the long trip to the wild and virtually unsettled central Texas.

This narrative will have to do with only one of the ten branches from the tree of Samuel and Amanda Brister who made the trip to Texas and eventually settled in Lampasas County.

True to the Scottish love for sheep, Grandpa Brister brought a few of his best with him. Grandma brought her spinning wheel and loom. The women and girls spent much of their time washing and combing the fiber into long strands for the spinning wheel, the yarn then turned into hopsacking on the loom which was used for everything from warm coats to saddle blankets. I still have a pair of Grandma's fiber combs. No one knows what happened to the spinning wheel.

Times on the frontier 1860 – 1900 were not easy. Friends and families stayed close and helped one another as they forged friendships with other refugees from the Civil War, seeking new beginnings in an unsettled area.

One such family was Mr. and Mrs. Dick Kolb, across the Colorado River in San Saba County.

In 1927 when our family relocated from west Texas to San Saba County, Daddy was thrilled to learn that Mr. and Mrs. Kolb lived in the community we had just moved into. They were approaching their 90s and we joined the others in the community calling them Grandpa and Grandma Kolb. Mr. Kolb died not long after we moved there, but we had a special bond with Grandma Kolb for as long as she lived. Sometimes when the family needed to be gone overnight they would ask me to spend the night with her; to gather the eggs, bring in firewood and a bucket of water. I loved to hear the stories she told, and sleep in that big soft feather bed.

Grandma Kolb was a first cousin to General Sam Houston. I was shocked when she expressed less than admiration for her first cousin, the hero I was studying about in Texas history. She said he was a "scoundrel". I think she was disappointed about his apparent love for a hard drink now and then.

Unfortunately, Grandpa Brister died in 1893, leaving Grandma with 10 children. My father, George Brister, was six years old. Some of the older children were already established in their own meager homes, but all joined in to care for Grandma and the younger children.

Daddy's oldest brother, Samuel (Uncle Buck) was the family idol and he took the responsibility for his little brother George.

When Daddy was about 16 and deemed to be a man ready for making it on his own, Uncle Buck provided the means for him to do it. So, he gave him one good horse and saddle, a pack mule, a good 30-30 rifle, twelve young ewes, and one ram along with the admonition, "Son, you take care of the sheep and they will take care of you." And they did.

SEARCHING

Another of Daddy's older brothers had already established a ranch in Iron County, an even more remote part of west Texas, so that became young George's destination.

Necessary provisions for the trip had to be light because they had to fit into the bed roll and a couple of saddle bags. A couple of cooking utensils for campfire cooking, a few staples like salt, sugar, coffee and flour. The land would have to provide other necessary food.

The little group pretty much followed the path of the rivers and streams to be near water. During rest stops for the tired animals Daddy had ample time to fish for dinner.

A campfire at night discouraged wild animals. The faithful watchdog would further alert Daddy should a wild animal approach with an apparent desire for a lamb dinner. The good rifle was always within reach for quick response when needed. The sheep were all pets by this time and preferred to bed down beside Daddy and the camp fire.

He arrived with his thirteen sheep at uncle S.T.'s ranch in about 1903. It had been a long slow journey across unoccupied open country.

Daddy and Uncle S.T. told many stories about the next few years (1908-1917), but unfortunately we did not record them and much has been forgotten. We do know that Daddy helped Uncle S.T. and devoted his time to developing his own flock.

When he was 17, Daddy joined one of the big cattle drives to Kansas City. We do not remember whether he told us they drove through to Kansas City or whether the cattle were put in rail cars someplace in Oklahoma and moved on to Kansas City. Apparently there was no wild stampede to add to the drama.

This period of history and the remoteness of the area contributed to a violent culture, because it was the perfect hideaway for the early outlaws, train robbers, and run of the mill gun slingers. The sheep men tending their flocks in the open range had less to fear from the outlaws than from possible hired killers sent to try to rid the country of the hated sheep. As a matter of fact, daddy once stated that he had met some "darn nice fellers" among the outlaws. One in particular he appreciated. One of the Ketchum brothers of the train robbing family (for whom the Ketchum Mountains are named) would stop by Daddy's camp now and then for a bit of conversation, a cup of coffee and share a meal of whatever Daddy had on a campfire, usually a pot of beans or some wild game. One day Mr. Ketchum came by to warn Daddy to keep a close watch because he had heard a certain hired gun in the area had a contract on him.

A few days later Mr. Ketchum came back and lifted the alert. It seems he had a chance run in with this hit man in a bar in Abilene and a slight misunderstanding resulted in the hit man losing the battle.

Sometimes a potential enemy could be one not suspected. One such individual was a deaf Indian everyone called "Dummy." This Indian had worked for Uncle S.T. off and on and he loved our Aunt Maud and their two little girls. Although he was deaf, they said it was impossible for anyone to slip up on him. He did surveillance work for several of the cattle ranchers. If there were cattle rustlers in the area, Dummy was the first to know. He could be hired to eliminate some of those rustlers and maybe a sheep man now and then.

One Christmas Aunt Maud took the two little girls on a trip to her mother's. While she was away, Daddy, his best friend, Emerson Cox, and a few men working the ranch were all at Uncle S.T.'s.

They all became violently ill – too sick to take care of one another. Someone came by, found the sick men, and sent a telegram to Aunt Maud to come home at once.

On the day she was to arrive in Barnhart, Daddy was the only one who could muster enough strength to hook a team to his wagon, take some warm blankets, and go meet the family. While he was at the depot daddy saw Dummy near the train stop so he knew Aunt Maud and the children got off the train.

As they approached the ranch house that evening, they saw Dummy's great white stallion fleeing the premises. When they entered the house, the first thing they observed was an empty baking powder can sitting on the wood cook stove. The contents had been dumped into the cold wood ashes. Aunt Maud scooped up some of it and they had it tested. It was almost pure arsenic. The doctors said the only reason that all who ate the biscuits did not die was the fact that the massive overdose had made them so ill that most of it kept coming up. Everyone knew that, without a doubt, Dummy had put the arsenic in the baking powder, knowing that hot baking powder biscuits were a staple of ranch life. He did not want Aunt Maud and the children harmed so he hurried back to the ranch to get rid of it. It was dumb for him to simply dump it in the wood stove and leave the empty can as evidence, but he had a simple mind. After all, his name was "Dummy."

Not long after that, someone murdered Dummy. The authorities called all surrounding ranchers, including Daddy and

Uncle Emerson Cox, before a grand jury seeking to find who killed Dummy. The consensus of all who were there was they did not know who killed him, but all were ever so grateful to whoever did. End of investigation.

Not long after Dummy's murder, a rumor circulated that authorities had found forty saddles in his attic. Apparently, he had no compulsion about killing a man or his horse, but he just could not abandon a good saddle.

Land was available for homesteading and Daddy chose one of the most remote areas on the Middle Concho River. He built a little shack on it which was to become our family's first home. We lived there when not following the "grazing trail."

A couple of the grazing excursions give a little insight into what it was like at this period of our history.

Our father was not a public speaker, a politician, nor one considered a church leader. He led by example. His word was his bond and everyone knew it. His policy was that your good name is the richest blessing a man could have and something money could not buy. A heritage of a good name was the birthright he expected to pass on to his children and each was charged to protect it and pass it on.

As children, we did not realize it, but as I have matured through several decades and made my own efforts for a closer walk with God, I have come to realize our father had a better understanding and unfailing faith than any of us realized. Through many years of hardship as a child and young man, he learned to read nature in a way few ever master.

Caring for his sheep, sleeping under the stars out on the open range, sometimes miles from another human, he had ample time to commune with God and nature.

The Mesquite tree–love it or hate it.

For one thing, he felt the eradication of the mesquite trees in the flats of west Texas was a mistake. How many knew that during hot, dry weather, those trees give off a fine spray of mist about two o'clock each morning. That big spray of moisture sustained the growth of lush mesquite grass under the trees that protected the soil and provided grass for animals. True, the trees drank the water, but they gave it back as a beautiful example of God's way to provide for His creatures of nature.

Daddy once told me that he had often observed this miracle when the dew fell so early in the morning. Suddenly there would appear small creatures of all kinds—rabbits, lizards, bugs, spiders, all to lap a drink from the grass. After their drink, they would frolic in the cool for a short while and just as suddenly as they had appeared, they would vanish from sight, back under the grass, into the soil, into their underground spots of safety.

One of his folklore stories that had to do with mesquite trees was another example of God's care for His animals. Everyone knows that sometimes these trees have very few beans and in other years the trees will be bending with a heavy load of the long sweet pods.

Daddy's theory was that come fall and the trees had that heavy crop, "look out, a hard winter was ahead." He was usually right. God was again providing food for the animals' winter foraging.

In 1917, Daddy returned to Lampasas County to visit his mother and other family. He was sporting a new Model-T and felt he was ready to settle into becoming a real rancher, and needed a wife and cook.

Uncle Buck, who had taken care of Daddy as a child and set him on the road to independence, had married Mother's oldest sister. When the two families got together for the holiday occasion and Daddy met Jessie Fox, it was love at first sight. He just could not return to the banks of the Middle Concho until he could secure a commitment from her to be his wife.

They were married March 17, 1918. Shortly thereafter Uncle Sam required Daddy's service for World War I and late that summer he departed for France. Mother came back to stay with Grandma Fox and her younger brother and sister and tried to keep the farm going.

On a bitter cold January 28, 1919, I made my arrival, weighing in at three pounds, two ounces, and to all accounts a horrible looking baby.

The awful story circulated among family was that mother took one look at me, turned her face to the wall and cried bitter tears.

Grandma Fox was my first guardian angel. She insisted that I had every potential to become a beautiful baby – I just needed to grow a bit. She bundled me in warm blankets and took me to bed with her, keeping me warm and feeding me with an eye dropper and covering my head while encouraging mother to nurse me.

As Grandma predicted, come spring flowers, the baby bloomed too and Mother consented to have her picture made with me. She was pleased to present me at age six months to Daddy upon his return from France.

Soon afterward, Daddy took Mother and me and returned to West Texas to take up where he had left off. Uncle S.T. and his helpers had faithfully cared for Daddy's flock and carefully counted all the increase into his inventory.

In 1921 George and Jessie's second child arrived, a baby boy who died as a newborn. He became one of the very first to be buried in what is now a large and beautiful ranchland cemetery in Mertzon, Iron County.

A WINTER IN FRONTIER
BIG BEND

The hot dry summer of 1923 was drawing to an end and there was no rain. The ground was bare of grass. Farming had not been introduced into this part of the west. Consequently, no grain or hay was available to sustain several thousand hungry sheep through the winter, even had there been money to purchase a sufficient amount.

The solution? Daddy mounted his favorite saddle horse and started across the open range to the southwest in search of winter grazing. He found it in the Big Bend Mountains overlooking the Rio Grande.

Uncle S.T. and Daddy combined their resources and the herds and prepared for the long slow move to the mountains. The big covered wagon was packed with a big tent to provide shelter, a wood cook stove for preparation of food and warmth for the tent, essential clothing, bedding, and most important, food. The bare necessity in food to last a few months was canned goods, flour, salt and pepper, molasses, coffee, sugar, lard, beans, rice, and salt pork. The land and streams would have to provide the rest.

Daddy acted as scout, going ahead each day mapping out the goal of travel for the next day, usually near the next source of water, and the easiest overland movement of the wagon and the Model-T driven by Mother. Uncle S.T. and several trusted Mexican herders would carefully lead the sheep in the path directed by the scout.

The wagon with the supplies and Mother with two small children usually reached the day's destination hours ahead of the herders and the flocks, The first thing that mother and the man handling the supply wagon (he was also the company cook) did was put a pallet beneath the big wagon as protection from the wild range cattle that would gather later for water. The cattle were curious and not always friendly.

For me, the most memorable thing that happened on this trip occurred on a hot day as we neared our destination. Even though I was not quite five years old, to this day I have a vivid picture of that vision before me. The sheep were taking their midday rest, Mother was preparing the family lunch, and Daddy was going to take a walk among the flocks to check their health and calm any that were restless. He was carrying A.J. and I was following along in the rough trail behind him.

Suddenly there arose out of a bush beside the trail the strangest snake imaginable. I think I stood immobilized for a short time as this creature waved his head back and forth in front of my face. No doubt, my angel snapped me out of my trance enough for me to scream.

Daddy came back to check on me, but the creature had probably slithered into the thick brush and Daddy did not spend a lot of time looking for it, possibly because he thought my description of what I had seen seemed a child's wild imagination. He knew a slow rattlesnake would still be very near and besides I knew a rattlesnake when I saw one. I described this one as having a long bill like a chicken, wearing a gray bonnet and he was pecking at me.

Years later I saw a documentary on TV that perfectly described this rarest of rare snakes and the world's most deadly one. They were known to have lived in the northern Mexico area, just across the river near the spot where we were. It resembled the Indian cobra and I could see where my description could be pretty accurate from a small child's perspective. Had his peck been a strike, my life would have lasted a maximum of three minutes. I guess God did not want to leave me in an unmarked grave high in that wilderness.

The winter months were cold and the wind always blew. A lot of details are a faint memory, but I do remember a wire fence Daddy put up around our tent to keep me in and the sheep out. To provide personal privacy for mother and me, a small tent was set up as our outhouse. Because it was so cold, they lined the tent with furs that the Mexican herders turned into rugs. They were good at processing the furs which would be sold once we returned to civilization. I am sure I was the only kid on that cold frontier that had a mink potty seat.

Spring rains had brought grass back at our home base. High March winds in the mountains blew our tent down so it was time to make the long trip back to Iron County and our home on the Middle Concho.

The only thing I remember about that trip was a blizzard that hit while we were in a very remote area. We were camped near a big water tower where big steam engines pulling the trains stopped for water.

Our bed was inside the covered wagon. When I peeped out in the morning I saw icicles that reached from the top of that water tower to the ground.

Little firewood was available in this area to build a warm fire. There was ample coal along the railroad track and Daddy had gathered a few sticks and a pile of coal. Good for cooking, but not much for warmth because it burned hot near the ground with lots of smoke that burned my eyes. I hated it because as I circled the fire, the smoke followed me.

Daddy eased that complaint somewhat when he explained that smoke always follows beauty and that I was beautiful, so that old smoke just had to follow me. A little unkempt urchin probably would have been a much better description. It was too cold to dip me in a stock tank for a bath, so a few cups of water in a washbasin had to do.

It was probably on this trip that I was introduced to Daddy's recipe for health, and may explain why I still like burned toast.

CHARCOAL FOR WHAT AILS
(George Brister's Recipe for Health)

Be careful of the water you drink. If in doubt, boil it and as an extra precaution, take a burning log from the campfire (preferably mesquite) and submerge it into the water. Of course little chunks of the charcoal and ash are left in the water, but strain the water through a clean flour sack cloth. It may not taste so good, but if you are thirsty, who cares. At least there are no germs.

I do not remember any of us ever being ill. Theory: Eat the charcoal and put nature's greatest purifying system directly where needed, in the stomach.

OLD CHARLIE LOSES HIS HALO

About the year 1925 Daddy leased land out near Rankin for grazing. He spent daylight to dark out on the range with the flocks. Mother was confined with my brother, A.J., and me in the shack that sat in a sea of greasewood brush and cacti, surrounded by only a lone windmill, a few stockade type corrals and watering troughs. Her only diversion was keeping an eye on us and some-times the flock of rams that were confined in a small fenced area surrounding the shack and near the water.

Daddy's favorite ram was a big beautiful animal named Charlie. Apparently Old Charlie decided he was unhappy and would take out his grievance on Mother. Consequently, she always carried a mesquite club about the size of a baseball bat when she went outside the yard. One day I got out of the yard and headed for the water troughs. Old Charlie saw me and came trotting. Mother, with her club came running to save me, yelling for me to lie down on the ground. The nature of sheep was that they would not attack a person who was down, but frozen in my tracks, I did not prostrate myself, so Charlie did it for me before Mother got to me. The result was a few scratches and bruises.

Somehow Mother got Charlie into a pen and locked the gate. When Daddy got home that evening he wanted to know why Charlie was locked up with no feed or water. Mother told him, in no uncertain terms, that old Charlie had to go. Daddy refused to believe that sweet old Charlie would harm anyone.

The next morning Daddy was down near the pens within Charlie's territory, mother was preparing breakfast when she heard a terrible commotion from that direction, accompanied by a flow of language seldom heard from the gentle shepherd. Mother ran down to see what was happening and found daddy holding old Charlie by one of his beautiful horns and beating him with a good sized club. She knew immediately what had happened and began to laugh and called to Daddy, "Don't hurt old Charlie. Remember, he won't hurt a fly."

Charlie had caught him not looking and hit him just below the knees, taking most of the skin off both shins with the prized set of horns. When it was over, daddy limped to the shack and admitted, "Yes, old Charlie had to go."

MIDNIGHT SURGERY

Daddy took Mother back to San Saba to the care of Grandma Fox and our beloved country Dr. Taylor for the birth of both A.J. and Eugene. I was too young to remember much about those stays, except I remember Eugene arrived on Easter Sunday and my uncles teased me they we were going to name him Easter Sunday and I cried about that prospect.

The one incident from that stay at Grandmas was this little girl, anxious to go barefoot on the first warm spring day, went out and promptly stepped on a very large mesquite thorn that penetrated deep within my foot. When the thorn was removed part of it, along with dirt from the barnyard, stayed in the wound, resulting in a serious infection. All the known home remedies to encourage the wound to drain failed. Finally, Uncle Tommy said surgery was the only answer and the family agreed.

About midnight, Grandma's beautiful dining table was turned into an operating table. There was a beautiful gas light chandelier above the table and someone was appointed to hold an oil burning lamp for added light. Uncle Tommy put a razor sharp edge on the long blade of his pocket knife, Grandma boiled the knife, and then the blade was held in the flame of the oil lamp. All was ready and this screaming child was placed in the middle of that dining table. Four people were assigned to hold me perfectly

still and Uncle Tommy split the wound. Out popped the re-
mainder of the thorn along with the accumulation of the infection. Pain relief was almost instantaneous to the great happiness
of all concerned. My foot was securely bandaged in a generous
helping of sugar soaked with turpentine. Healing was complete
and prompt.

As we were returning to west Texas with the newborn baby
brother, a big wasp flew into the open car and stung the baby on
the forehead. Naturally, the baby screamed and mother's emo-
tions were out of control. Even before Daddy could stop the car,
he bit the end off the cigar he had in his mouth and handed it to
Mother to put on the sting. After all, in an emergency, you use
whatever first aid is available. I guess it worked, because within
a few minutes all was well and the baby seemed no worse from
the sting.

Following the return home on Middle Concho with the new
second son, George and Jessie realized there could be no more
grazing ventures with the flocks and if another drought hit, they
would have to depend on God to provide the answer. Their
thoughts then turned toward turning this remote area into a
home. More barns and corrals were added, along with a garden
spot, chickens, a couple of turkey hens, and a gobbler. Mother
wanted the assurance we could have Thanksgiving and Christmas
dinners just as people in the civilized world. Most of all, her
dream came true when daddy presented her with a fine Jersey
milk cow. The range cows, even if raised from calves, could never
be trained to be gentle creatures and their milk was devoid of
cream to make butter. Old Jersey was a beloved member of our
family for years to come. Not only did she provide milk and
butter for our family and cottage cheese for baby chickens and
turkeys, but ample milk for orphan baby lambs and calves that
had to be bottle fed.

Just a few incidents from the next couple of years are recorded
partly from memory, but mostly from retelling by parents. The

area was remote and lonely, especially for the few women in the country.

Our nearest neighbors were our parent's dearest friends, fondly known to us as Uncle Emerson and Aunt Mable Cox and their children. Their ranch was about 25 miles away so our visits were not that frequent, but something always cherished by both families. One such visit was memorable.

A COLD MARCH WIND AND SAN-ITIZED KIDS

It was March and the spring stock show was being held at San Angelo where the ranchers gathered to bargain for new and improved breeding stock. Daddy and Uncle Emerson were going to enjoy the diversion together. Mother and children were delivered to the Cox ranch early in the morning for a day and night of fun for the kids and a wonderful visit of two young mothers who longed for the rare association of another woman.

When we arrived, Aunt Mable was already involved in wash day. The big iron kettles were filled with boiling water, the wash tubs, rub board, and lye soap were all ready, and mother was delighted to join in the fun of putting out a big laundry as the two visited. Their daughter, Nina Lee, and I were the same age and we were left to find our own entertainment. Our first venture was to the barn where a very gentle old saddle horse was kept especially for the children. We led the gentle horse up beside something we could climb upon and thus mount the horse bareback. We did not get very far on that ride until I slid off the animal's back side. No way to remount without anything to climb on, so we returned to the barn to see what other adventure we could find.

An old Mexican ranch hand lived in a tent down by the barn. We decided that would be a good place to play out of the March wind. It proved to be true until a couple of mothers decided to check on us. They were horrified to find us in that tent. They were sure we were thoroughly infested with all kinds of vermin, so two little girls were escorted to the back yard, stripped bare, clothes washed out and dumped into the boiling water, two heads dipped in a pan of kerosene then shampooed with the lye soap. After the scrub down, we were dressed in a couple of uncle Emerson's long sleeved undershirts and made to sit by the fireplace to dry our hair while our clothes flapped in the breeze on the long clothes lines stretched from one mesquite tree to another.

It's a wonder we did not catch our death of colds, but the rugged ranch life that afforded few creature comforts produced healthy children.

EGGS TO MARKET

On another spring day, Daddy was going to make a trip to either Mertzon or Barnhart.. Mother's hens were happy and she had two or three dozen eggs on hand so she decided to send some to market, knowing fresh eggs were a real treat at the local grocery. She knew the proceeds would pay for a couple of yards of gingham to make a new dress for the ragged little daughter.

Daddy took the eggs without comment, but for someone who considered himself to be a fairly successful rancher, the idea of marketing eggs did not fit the profile he wished to project.

He did bring back the gingham, but it was sometime later that Mother learned that he had stopped in "shanty town," called some little Mexican children and presented them with some fresh eggs.

A SHOPPING TOUR THAT
GAINED A PRECIOUS MEMORY

After I was an adult, Mother told me about a rare shopping experience she had on one of the trips she made to San Angelo with Daddy. While he attended to business elsewhere, she planned to enjoy shopping at San Angelo's major department store, Hemphill Wells. She said a very beautiful salesperson accompanied her throughout the store and was very helpful.

When she completed her shopping, mother wrote a check to pay for the purchases. The saleslady looked at the check and said, "Brister, do you happen to know a rancher named George Brister?" With her usual sense of humor, mother replied, "Well, I hope I know him, I'm his wife."

The lady was dumbfounded. She said, "Well, I guess that explains a lot of things and I want you to know right now that you must be one of the luckiest people in the world." She went on to explain that Daddy had been in that store many times through the years and she considered him the most handsome man ever to set foot in there and that she had used every trick she knew to attract his attention. She said that he was the only man she ever saw from whom she could not elicit a second glance.

This saleslady's comments were a real morale builder and a memory that lived in a secret corner of a heart for as long as it beat – 98 years.

FAMILY SECURITY—A BIG BLACK GREYHOUND NAMED RACER

The days of unfriendly Indians were already history during the 1920s, but for women alone during long days, it had to be a terrifying experience at times. Caution had to be observed every moment. Rattlesnakes, wild animals, unfriendly wild cattle were minor fears. Then, as now, there were humans, seeking a better life, making their way through unpopulated country. Since our home was located near the river, it was naturally in the path that some of these strangers followed. On rare occasions the strangers were known to ask for or simply take food for themselves or their horses from any ranch house along the way. Women were always petrified when strange men approached, and Mother was no exception.

Soon after their marriage, Daddy had taught Mother to become a crack shot with a new rifle he provided for her protection.

In addition, we were blessed to have the best guard dog that ever lived. Uncle S.T. had rescued a pair of blue ribbon greyhound racers from the dog racing tracks near Del Rio. He had given us a puppy from the pair. Racer was tall, powerful, completely devoted, and most protective for our family for over 19 years. She never barked, but if Daddy was not home no human or animal dare come within 100 feet of the yard, day or night. Mother had to signal her that it was OK before anyone was allowed to enter the yard or dismount from their horse.

There was only one occasion when mother relied on Racer for real protection. Daddy had gone to Mertzon for supplies. Late in the evening, Mother, the three of us, and Racer were out near the barns checking on some animals that were being kept near the barns for special care. She saw two men walking up the road from the river area, so with the children and the dog she hurried to the house, bringing Racer with us through the back door. She hurried to lock the front screen door about the time the men reached the yard. Racer was having a fit to get to them. One of the men called to Mother, "We come for tobacco." She explained there was no tobacco, which was the truth because Daddy had left with the last pipe full of pipe tobacco. The fact that the pipe tobacco tin was empty had triggered the need to go for supplies on this day.

The men stepped up on the porch and said, "We come in to see." Whereupon mother warned that she was going to release the dog and reached for the door latch. As Racer charged out, both men made a leap to the big mesquite tree in the yard. Fortunately for them, there was a low limb that provided a quick hoist for higher limbs slightly above the dog's reach, but she was not going to allow them to come down. This enabled Mother to be a little braver, so she stepped out with the loaded rifle and advised that she would call the dog off long enough for them to get away but if they ever came back she would allow the dog to cut their throats, which is what she would have done. Mother said she never knew men could run so fast. Racer was most disappointed that she was denied the opportunity to attack.

DECISIONS, DECISIONS

Yes, another baby was on the way late in 1926. Apparently Mother and Daddy felt they were brave enough to face this arrival out in no man's land. One of daddy's sisters, Aunt Ida Smith, came to stay with us to help with mother and care for A.J., Eugene, and me. She had a great sense of humor and we loved having her.

The arrival of this third baby brother on April 27, 1927, demanded of our parents some soul-searching about the future. I was school age. Mother had been trying to home school me with inadequate help, plus the fact that to cope with all the challenges was simply too much for a young mother. Four young children, cooking, housekeeping, laundry with the wash tubs and rub board, cows to milk, chickens, turkeys, a garden, and often Daddy needed help to accomplish something.

What to do? Did they want to establish a second home in either Mertzon or Barnhart for Mother and children during school months and leave Daddy on the ranch as most families did? The only other option seemed to be to make a complete change and seek a home in a part of the state that had rural schools that would make it possible for families to stay together and still follow the only known way to make a living – ranching.

Mother and Daddy were completely devoted to each other and with a pending big family, it was obvious that would mean many years of school age children. They were not willing to face years of a split household.

Where to look? Relatives from both parents still lived in both San Saba and Lampasas counties, so we went on a vacation to Grandma Fox's farm in San Saba to give Daddy a chance to go ranch shopping. I have no idea of how he found the spot on Rough Creek, which was in the most remote wilderness part of the entire county; I believe the local banker took him to see it. Daddy apparently saw great possibilities and made a deal. That fact alone reflects a great change in the culture of the last century. I am sure it did not occur to either of them to take Mother on these shopping tours. I am convinced that had she been there the day Daddy visited this canyon, we would not have ended up on Rough Creek.

While they lived in West Texas, the nearest big town was San Angelo. For their big shopping, banking, and marketing the wool, they visited San Angelo. Spending a night or two in a hotel and eating out at Daddy's favorite grill was the thrill of a lifetime.

San Angelo was then, and remains, the wool capital of the USA. Daddy, uncle S.T., and Emerson Cox were proud to have helped to make it so.

My only sister grew up and married the son of a pioneer railroad family in San Angelo, Bill Herman. Bill and Mary Evelyn raised a wonderful family, one son and three daughters. This family has kept alive the pride of our Concho Valley heritage.

Citizens of the area are proud of their beautiful Concho River, north, south, and middle. The special Concho pearls grow in all three rivers. This is the only place in the world where they grow in the quality and colors that range in shades from pink, purple, orchid, and copper.

Japan tried to reproduce cultured pearls in those colors but it could not be done. Japan then tried to lease the lakes so they could raise the pearls, but west Texas likes "nature's way" and chose not to let it happen.

There has been a lot of harvesting of the pearls, but now a license is required to look for them and only limited amounts can be taken. They are becoming rare.

Because of the significance of the middle Concho in our heritage, Bill and Evelyn had a 14k gold necklace cast in the shape of Texas and one of the Concho pearls mounted about the site of our home on the middle Concho. Isn't it strange, like the Concho pearl this incredible family with some of the same uniqueness both originated in the Concho Valley?

THE ROUGH CREEK SHOCK

The decision was made and the contract signed on a wilderness spot in San Saba County; the family hurried back to the ranch on the Middle Concho. Much had to be done. Sell the land, choose the best from the flocks daddy wanted to keep, and deliver them to the safekeeping at uncle S.T.'s ranch, sell the rest, sell the wool stored in warehouses in San Angelo, and make arrangements with the railroad for boxcars and transportation of cargo and animals to their new home. At this period in history, Texas had a better railroad system than highways. There was not a mile of pavement in west or central Texas

All household possessions were packed into big wagons that had served as home on the range in the various grazing ventures. This expedited the move at the end of the line because they could remove the loaded wagon from the rail car, hitch the team, and proceed to Rough Creek.

The team of horses that pulled the wagon and did heavy work, Daddy's two favorite saddle horses, Mother's fine jersey milk cow, and a few young heifers were in stock cars. Two of the heifers belonged to A.J. and me. Daddy had rescued the newborn calves that had been abandoned in one of the spring roundups from adjoining ranches. He gave each of us one of the calves with the stipulation that we were to care for them. Old Jersey gave ample milk for all concerned and we bottle fed our little pets until they could drink milk from a bucket.

Income from the increases provided by these young heifers was sometimes the only source of funds for a new Easter outfit in the spring and back to school clothes in the fall.

It was mid-August of 1927, the temperature was 110 degrees, and the family left ahead of the train, traveling in a model-T touring car for the long hot trip to San Saba. Today's travel time would be approximately two hours. Our trip was more like twelve hours. A.J. and I, along with Racer, occupied the back seat. Mother took care of Eugene, age 2, and Rayford, 4 months. A small trailer with precious cargo was hitched to the back of the model-T. Its cargo was a 300-pound, very pregnant sow. She was special because she represented the future major food supply of bacon, ham, sausage, and lard. Because it was so hot, mother and daddy were concerned for the sow's safety. Fortunately all the villages along the way did have ice houses and they were the stops of first choice. Daddy would get 100 pound blocks of ice and put around the mother hog to keep her straw wet and somewhat protect her from the heat. The family also craved the ice. Mother kept damp towels spread over the baby.

As soon as we arrived in San Saba, Daddy delivered an exhausted family, dog, and mother hog to Grandma Fox's farm and he went to wait for the train and arrange for help to move cargo and animals to Rough Creek. The fine details of just how that was accomplished are not clear in my memory, but I do know the team pulled the big wagon and daddy contracted local help and wagons to transport other goods and animals. The saddle horses were ridden by the Mexican ranch hands who had accompanied the animals in the boxcars.

The big shock was when Daddy finally brought Mother and kids to the new home. A.J. and I were terrified. All our lives we had lived in open country, and this was a canyon with high rock cliff on one side of the creek and a forest on the other.

It was a beautiful valley; however, the real beauty was hidden at this time. Huge pecan trees, oaks, and cedar plus all kinds of brush made it a forest. The creek was overgrown with a solid stand of willow that grew like bamboo. The people who lived there had neglected everything. The beautiful mountain spring that had supplied water to the area for centuries was all but lost in the growth.

All water for household use had to be transported by bucket to the house, a distance of perhaps 100 feet. The previous occupants had taken string and tied the high weeds back from the trail to the spring. Mother wondered how much less energy that required than taking a hoe and clearing a path.

There were several log barns and cribs in various stages of falling down. All were filled with junk from years of neglect and old hay and corn no longer fit for animal food. The house was newer, but still less than desirable.

What could George Brister possibly have seen in this place?

The family living there should have been gone when we arrived. Camping out was our option, so Mother and Daddy cleared a spot on the creek bank surrounding the spring of weeds and trash. They put the wagon in the middle, unloaded the wood cook stove, and set it up beside one of the big pecan trees, set up the iron beds, and covered them with heavy mosquito nets.

The night time was especially terrifying for A.J. and me. It was dark under those trees and the symphony of the night sounds was unbelievable. Crickets singing, screech owls in the trees screeching, the great horned owls on the bluff calling, "who, who" and the never-ending wonk, wonk of the big bull frogs that lived in the creek. We much preferred the howl of the coyote in west Texas.

I know Mother was totally disenchanted, but it was not in her nature to give up. It had been her dream to get back to an area of schools, churches, and neighbors within visiting distance, so then and there she was dedicated to help Daddy turn this jungle into a home.

The second night, as Mother was preparing supper on the wood cook store, Daddy's beautiful black and white paint saddle horse came up and nudged her on the shoulder. She encouraged him to move away, but he was immediately back. This time she looked at him because he seemed to be seeking attention. Instantly she could see that he had been snake bitten on the side of his face. Paint had been wading in the cool water below the spring and enjoying the lush green stuff growing there. Many big water moccasins lived there.

Paint had been bitten by a large rattlesnake in west Texas and mother and daddy had spent two days and nights by his side in a battle to save his life. No doubt, Paint remembered. Once again this couple spent a long night nursing a favorite animal and once more he survived.

Where to begin to make a home in this strange land? The Mexican helpers who had helped with the move had returned to west Texas. The community was made up of descendants of earlier settlers, most of whom were related one way or another and all were very suspicious of outsiders.

Perhaps out of curiosity about what this young upstart who arrived with family and animals was up to, several neighbors came and volunteered help. After all, this was a potential addition to the country school and the Methodist church that was central to the Colony community.

Grades at the two room school ended at the eighth grade and that was the end of education for most. Daddy was delighted to find that Grandma Kolb lived in this community. That was a connection that reached back to his parents. The next family who became fast friends was the Dee Towerton family. Their teenage son, Clayton (always fondly known as Smokey) became Daddy's right hand in everything that had to be done.

Those Brister kids had to be introduced into the school and Sunday School for the first time and eventually the community accepted us as their own.

The first thing to be accomplished was to repair some temporary fences around the valley to keep the animals with us nearby. The second goal was to build the large barn for shelter for animals and storage area for animal feed, salt and machinery. Corrals would have to be built surrounding the big barn.

The third goal was to get a goat-proof net wire fence around the entire ranch. The adjoining ranches had cattle and three-wire barbed wire fences pretty well kept them where they needed to be. Barbed wire fence would be no help in keeping sheep and goats on their own property. Daddy knew he would have to convert mostly to goats because of the impossible growth of brush and solid stand of a virgin cedar. Sheep liked grass off the ground; goats liked leaves from the branches as high as they could climb.

A visit to each adjoining property owner seeking help with the expense of providing the net wire fence met with some skepticism, but one neighbor agreed to pay his half for the wire that adjoined his ranch. All pledged labor to get it done which greatly expedited the process of getting the fence in place.

The first hard winter was consumed with getting settled, construction of barns, corrals, chicken house, pig pens, and clearing a spot for Mother's spring garden.

In early summer, Daddy returned to west Texas to move his sheep that were left behind. Once again, they came by train and this time Daddy rode in the boxcar with the sheep to assure their safety. He also brought with him the new machine-powered shearing clippers that had come on the market. This greatly expedited the process of taking the wool and mohair. He taught

Smokey Towerton and some other local boys how to use the machines and they soon became professionals and were in much demand. He still needed better grazing for the sheep, but the valley and small fenced areas near the creek provided for a limited number of sheep. Daddy had purchased 600 angora goats and they were happily making headway on the brush.

It was September 1928, and another winter was approaching. The shearing was done and Daddy took his new shearing rig and newly trained helpers to help some other ranchers in the area who had goats. Their first job was about fifteen miles away so they stayed at the ranch.

It was the first day of school. We had to be up early to get to school, a three-mile walk. Daddy had stored several cans of kerosene in an old smokehouse near the house. On the night before school was to start, mother had asked me to bring a can of the kerosene into the house so she could start a quick fire in the wood stove the next morning. As children often do, I promptly forgot it until I heard her get up the next morning so I jumped up to get it for her.

My guardian angel warned me at the door not to go in, but I pushed that fear aside, telling myself it was because I just always felt fear of dark spots. As I came through the door, I knew a rattlesnake had bitten me and I screamed that fact to Mother who came running, but did not want to believe it. She brought an oil lamp, shined it inside and saw nothing, so she stepped inside carrying the lamp in one hand and a garden hoe in the other. As she turned to come back, she saw the snake poised ready to get her as well. She killed the snake and came to check on me. I was already soaking my foot in the kerosene I had brought with me. There was no doubt I had been bitten. Swelling was already progressing up my leg. We had no phone.

Our nearest neighbor, the Parkers, lived a little over a mile away. Mother wrote Mrs. Parker a note to call the doctor and Daddy, and sent A.J., age 7, to take it to her. The little fellow ran all the way. Mrs. Parker made the calls and then they brought A.J. home and stayed with us the rest of the day and night. Our faithful Dr. Taylor, who had delivered me, arrived as soon as his Model-T could get him there, which was pretty soon.

The new serum for rattlesnake bites had come on the market and Dr. Taylor brought one with him. My leg had swollen to my hip and I was a very, very ill little girl. Daddy and Smokey had arrived by the time the doctor arrived and several neighbors came and most of them spent the entire day and night. I guess they felt that my parents should not be alone if they lost me. Dr. Taylor came and went all day and night doing what he could. When it was decided I would live, everyone went home, but this incident delayed my start to school by six weeks.

We Brister kids had never been around other children other than our own family, and so had never been exposed to childhood conflicts. Consequently, it took some effort to integrate into this closely knit community. After school, walks up the country road seemed the worse. The little school bully, Chat Hicks, seemed to take delight in picking on my seven-year old brother.

After a few days of our coming home crying about this, Mother sat us down and explained that it was time for us to learn to take care of ourselves. We took the idea to heart. The next afternoon when Chat hit A.J., I came to his defense and Chat hit me. That did it. I had a new green metal lunch basket in which Mother had placed something in a heavy cup. It made a good weapon and I hit Chat in the head with it, resulting in a knot on his head and a bent all-out-of-shape lunch basket.

The next morning the teacher kept all of us in at morning recess to settle the question of the fight the day before. She asked me, "What did my mother think of a little girl hitting a boy?"

I told the truth: "She said, 'Next time get a good stick and don't ruin your lunch basket.'"

I do not remember whether the teacher laughed, but she did excuse all of us and I am sure she saw the humor in the whole thing. Later and through our teen years, Chat was a good friend.

A little side story to the shearing rig. It is hard to describe, but there were metal frames from which all sorts of belts and pulleys powered the clippers. The whole thing was powered by a gasoline engine attached to the master pulley. That old engine, purchased in 1928 to power that original shearing rig is still in use, granted only after one of my brothers, Jack, had it rebuilt at considerable expense. Through the depression years of the 1930s, war years of the 1940s and beyond, that old engine pulled the grist mill, the pump to irrigate the garden, the orchard, and the ribbon cane patch to provide the finest of cane for the best home-made molasses, the big circle saw to cut firewood for the cook stove and the fireplace during the winter, and anything else that needed power.

When Jack had the old engine refurbished, he also had the old grist mill repaired. He enjoys setting it up on special occasions and everyone loves the wonderful corn meal it produces. Each summer, at family reunions on Rough Creek, Jack brings the special trailer on which the old engine and grist mill are mounted and the great-grandchildren witness a bit of history and enjoy the pop, pop of that grand old engine that once more echoes in the valley on Rough Creek.

Work continued through that second winter and Daddy was looking forward to a happy time in March when the new baby lambs were to arrive. He had planned well. The big barn was ready to shelter if the weather was bad. As always, unexpected things happen to farmers and ranchers.

When we described the general state of decay of the place when we first arrived, we did not include a trouble spot that was not suspected. The original early settlers had established corral of stone, simply stacking loose lime rocks that lay in abundance one on another. Probably wire was not available and they did not elect to do rail fences. The loose stones were without a doubt good when they were put here, but they had long since become piles of stone rubble. Unfortunately much of this rubble was near where the big barn had been placed. Little did my parents know that these piles of stones provided home to hundreds of the big wood rats that never show their faces in daylight, but appeared at night. When baby lambs were born, they were attacked by the rats. The mothers were incapable of protecting the young. Mother, Daddy, Smokey and the dog worked throughout the night trying to save the baby lambs from the hungry hordes.

Daddy rushed to town, purchased 30 pounds of fresh hamburger and a big can of KRO (Kick Rats Over) poison. Smokey went rabbit hunting to supplement the meat supply and the generous supply of food was put out. The next morning Daddy and Smokey picked up over 100 dead creatures and deposited them into a big log fire, but they forgot that probably hundreds more had returned into the rock piles. Consequently, within a few days the odor in the valley made life unbearable. Another massive cleanup job was in order. This huge undertaking had been delayed in the face of other tasks that seemed more pressing, but the time had come. Cedar trees and brush cut and piled on the rock rubble and a massive fire set not only to the brush piles, but the old barns, cribs and whatever else may have provided shelter for unwanted varmints and snakes. This massive cleanup took valuable time from other things, but it was worth the effort.

At last, George and Jessie Brister felt a bit secure. They could look at what had been accomplished, celebrate the arrival of a fourth son, and could begin plans for building a lovely new house for our growing family. But alas, it was not to be.

Without warning, the Great Depression arrived. Suddenly the goats purchased at $3 each could not be given away. Neither could the sheep nor the cattle. Wool and mohair sat in the warehouse. There was no money to meet bank notes. Fortunately the bankers knew and trusted Daddy, and they could do nothing with repossessed land and animals anyway. The bank could not sell them either, so they decided to leave it in the best hands to handle it.

Possibly because free range was disappearing across the west, and farms and ranches were putting the new net wire fences around property, the cedar posts and pickets were in demand and were about the only commodity the owners of these cedar forests had to sell.

Many displaced families seeking a living were happy to contract to clear the land of the cedar in exchange for the posts. Daddy was anxious to clear the land so grass could grow, so that cedar sustained several families through some hard years. He kept only a few cents from each post sold. It was not enough to help the bottom line but enough to keep the bank hopeful for a happy outcome.

The solid growth of willow that choked Rough Creek also was put to use by some of the resourceful people who camped along the creek. They wove willow baskets and made willow furniture. For years we had chairs and tables of willow. This depression furniture is all long since consigned to the trash, but would anyone guess what a good piece of it would be worth at an antique shop today?

In 1936, the San Saba school district decided that the poverty-stricken, culturally deprived students deserved the wonderful experience of a trip to the big city of Dallas to visit the Texas Centennial. Such a ragged bunch made the all-night train ride from San Saba to Dallas. It was undoubtedly a strange sight, but it was Mother and Daddy's decision that those children who lived in the tents along the creek should have this trip. Eugene, Rayford and I were asked to forgo any new clothes for that trip and Daddy took what little he could spare and bought each of those children some new clothes. For one little girl, it was the first store-bought dress she had ever had, and she was about as excited over that new dress as she was the trip.

The school district picked up expenses for children, teachers, and parents who came on the trip. Daddy gave me $20 for spending on myself and my two younger brothers, Eugene and Rayford. Would you believe we got home with $10 of that and souvenirs for everyone? Hamburgers, hot dogs, and other treats the big fair had to offer were only five or ten cents, so the kids did not go without treats.

Daddy made one prediction after we returned from that trip: He made the statement that he was sure I would grow up to become a millionaire because if I could take two little boys to a big fair like that with $20 and come home with $10, I had to be a good manager.

Many of the children of those families served in World War II, returned, got a good education, and became successful business people and farmers with their own property.

Through the years, the bread of compassion spread on the water of those in need came floating back in so many ways.

A COMMUNITY CANNING BEE

In 1933 and 1934, the Great Depression was still much a part of our lives. It was correctly named because everyone was depressed, but that did not keep the community of neighbors from banding together to enjoy life. The good country people did pull together to help one other and to share with the homeless families that migrated to the camp site along the streams where there was water, fish, and wild life that could be hunted for food.

This was before rural electricity, running water, or indoor plumbing. The winters were colder then and the summers just as hot.

Social security, welfare, and all other government assistance programs we know today were still in the future. As a matter of fact, there was a lot of grumbling that some of the work programs President Roosevelt pushed were wrong. The idea was that we were not supposed to feel the government was to care for us. But history does show that many of those programs not only helped to pull the nation from the grasp of the Depression, but advanced the quality of life and opportunity years ahead of where it may have gone at the rate it had been moving.

Without refrigeration, it was not practical for individual families to butcher animals during warm weather. The neighbors made a schedule of sharing the donation of animals. The men would meet, butcher and divide the meat, and everyone would eat "high on the hog" for a day or so.

Chickens, turkeys, milk, butter and eggs were always available to share, along with garden vegetables and corn fields with their endless rows of beans and peas planted between the rows of corn. About this time the new canning machines came on the market. We came to know big pressure cookers, tin cans with the lids and sealers to secure the lids just as the canned goods we obtain at our grocery today.

Mr. and Mrs. Dee Towerton were the first to invest in this new equipment and Mother and Daddy brought the second one into the Colony. All gardens were ready to harvest at the same time and some things like corn stayed at the peak of harvest for a very short time, so the community arranged weekly or bi-weekly canning sessions. Everyone took his or her produce to a given host family. A wood stove was set up under a shade tree in the yard to keep the pressure cookers going and the party would begin. A lot of visiting went on as the food was prepared, and fun was shared while everyone worked and a lot of cans were set aside for winter's food supply.

One of the most memorable of those canning bees occurred at what later became Daddy's farm, but it was then owned by two maiden sisters, Misses Betty and Mattie Jones. Miss Betty was the stronger of the two so she did the farming, with one mule and her walking plow. Miss Mattie was frail so she kept house and cared for a beautiful flower garden.

During the day, Miss Betty complained that she did not like these new canning machines and that the three-pound cans did not hold as much as the quart jars she was used to. Mr. Dee says, "Oh, Betty, this can hold exactly the amount of that jar." She was amazed that he could be so ignorant. He filled a can with water, handed it to her and said, "Here, pour it in that jar to measure." She did, and sure enough the measure was exactly the same.

Mr. Dee made one mistake. He threw his head back and laughed. In her rage, Miss Betty flung the can at him and the unsealed edge of that new can cut a ring around his entire face. His nose and mouth was a bloody center of the doughnut. At that, Daddy had to join in the laughter, but Miss Betty did not have anything handy to throw at him.

As the rest of the party stood in shock and someone brought wet towels for Mr. Dee's face, meek Miss Mattie came to Betty's defense with, "I don't care if Sister kills every old man in the county." All the men who were there laughed about that scene for years.

LINGERING DAYS OF
DEPRESSION ON ROUGH CREEK

As this family struggled along with the community and the rest of the country to survive the many obstacles, God always seemed to provide. By today's standards, we lived in poverty, but we did not know it because no neighbors or friends had more. There was love to share not only with family, but with neighbors and those truly in need. Those little Brister boys and their friends lived in a boy's paradise and watching them grow was our parent's greatest happiness.

Each Sunday morning mother was up extra early and before departure for Sunday School, dinner had been prepared for at least six to ten extra kids because all of them, along with parents, came home with us for lunch and afternoon swimming, fishing, or whatever else. Games of tossing horseshoes or softball were common. It was not uncommon that Mother would have fried at least five chickens for the hungry bunch. If too many for the long family table, they simply moved the food to tables under the big pecan trees on the creek bank.

Mother and Daddy both had a great sense of humor and the kids delighted in trying to put something over on them. Sometimes they were successful. One such incident happened when Mother found herself backed into a corner of her own declaration. The boys and three or four of their friends finished lunch and set up a howl for permission to go swimming. Daddy did not care, but Mother's answer was an adamant "No" because the water was still too cold and they would all get pneumonia and die. Then the question, "How long would it take them to get the dreaded pneumonia?" "Oh my," mother answers, "probably by tomorrow night all of you could be sick." With that, they all jumped up with a whoop, "Come on boys, we are safe." Seems they had all been in swimming the Sunday before and they had been waiting all week to see if any of them got sick. Daddy thoroughly enjoyed the shocked look on Mother's face.

There was never a time when we did not have food on the table. To be complete, the daily requirement was the big black cast iron pot of pinto beans. A fresh pot was put on the big wood cook stove each morning. One summer day, when the garden had all kinds of wonderful things to eat, Mother declared that she was going on strike. This family would eat something other than beans and she would not cook them.

This lasted about a week. One morning Mother saw four of those sons coming up the road. Two of them were half carrying Eugene and the others were walking as if injured. She was sure they had fallen off a cliff or out of a tree and someone was hurt so she dashed down the road to meet them.

"Oh no," was their answer. It was just that they had not had beans in so long that their legs had run out of starch. Mother said that if it was not so funny, she would have felt like killing them, but she agreed: "Oh well, go put a fire in the stove and I will put the bean pot on."

To accommodate a few of us, the school board had added the ninth grade to a two- room, two-teacher Colony school.

The report card read straight "A's" – promoted to the tenth grade.

This was the end of the cycle of education for most graduates of Colony and the other rural schools. Tears flowed because this ninth grader did not want to forgo what might lie beyond those canyons and the many more things school could reveal.

The distance to the new high school that San Saba was very proud of was not that far, only about 15 miles, but it may as well have been 50. The unpaved dirt road was almost impassable during the winter for the Model T Ford, too far for horseback and wagon and mules were out of the question.

My friend, Ione Chambliss, felt the same way as I did, so our parents decided they had to find a way for these girls to continue for a high school education.

Some friends from the community, John and Irene Harrell, had moved to town. They had a big old house down near the cotton gin. The depression had them, like almost everyone else, in near poverty, so they were happy to rent one big room to our parents for $3 or $4 per week, plus commodities from our sources (milk, butter, eggs, vegetables, etc.).

Come September, our parents furnished this room for us— a couple of cots, some nice apple boxes for book cases, a couple of old chairs, a homemade table with a new oil cloth cover, and most important, a small cast iron wood stove which was also to be our only source of warmth during the cold winter.

During school months, each Sunday evening, Daddy would deliver us to town, along with the week's supply of food and firewood. When school was out Friday evening, he would be waiting to return us to the country. Our social activities were limited to our rural churches and community activities. Those city kids did not see us on weekends.

We country kids were petrified to face the teachers at the new high school. Especially did we dread facing Mrs. Grace Henry, the lead English teacher who had a reputation of never having a student complete her classes and then fail an English course in college. Most avoided registering for her class, but I had decided to see what she was really like.

On the first day, I registered for Mrs. Henry's class and reported for orientation. I think I was the only new student she had not seen before, so she immediately confronted me with one harsh question. "What are you doing here?"

My upbringing had drilled me to be polite and respectful of teachers and helped me answer with what I hoped would be grace: "Here to take this English class."

She looked at my record from the Colony. Then, she says, "We have never had a student from the Colony. I doubt you can make it, so you probably do not belong in this class."

Needless to say, I was hurt, embarrassed, and dumbfounded, but this was my first real opportunity in the world of hard knocks to come, to practice "grace under fire." My father's calm sense of patience and independence came forth. My answer: "I've heard you are a tough but fair teacher, and I am willing to try this if you are."

What could she say?

My goal was to make it, whatever it took. She did not make it easy, and I had to work for it.

Mrs. Henry did not know that the Colony kids made up for their isolation with books. She could not know that my brother, A.J., and I had averaged reading about 200 books per year since the fifth grade. This included everything from the school's lending library, the county library, and all the books and magazines that friends, neighbors and relatives could possibly pass on to us.

The first six weeks was a disappointing B+, but the next three years were straight A's.

I do not think Mrs. Henry ever learned to love the country kids, but she was a great teacher who made even Shakespeare come alive.

She was fair and from her I learned to love not only the great literature, but the dangling participle and even the split infinitive.

WHAT NOW?

By 1938, depression still stalked the USA, and there were worries about the upheavals in Europe. What a time to face an unknown future.

In May of 1938, about 43 kids walked out of the San Saba High School gym, clutching beautiful diplomas, bound in purple real sheepskin leather, embossed in gold. We faced a troubled world that would become even more troubled— one that would take the lives of several of those who walked down the aisle and out that door.

My immediate concern was, "What now?" How can I continue my education? Mother and Daddy would love to send me to the university at Austin, my dream, but after several years of the Great Depression, and Daddy's desperate attempt to save the ranch while providing for the needs of an ever-growing family, there simply was no money. No one had thought of student loans.

I am confident that had I shown any great unhappiness about putting my dreams on hold, Daddy would have tried to move a few mountains in an effort to provide the means. I now suspect that Mother knew that and she tried hard to shield him from the heartbreak of disappointing me. She sat me down for a long and serious discussion of facts.

The general attitude of the surrounding culture was that higher education for girls was not nearly as important as that for the boys. Girls did not need a lot of book learning to become good mothers, cooks, housekeepers, and day laborers beside that good husband who was supposed to take care of them.

The facts outlined were:

Number one, there was no money and even if I worked for my room and board as much as possible, the family would have to sacrifice. Number two, there were now seven boys and one adorable little sister behind me and our parents needed to secure the future for the boys. I had no problem with that. Number three, they would help me search for a career a girl could pursue that they could afford. Opportunities for women were limited

Some hospitals were offering nurses' training with financial benefits and we had about settled into following that course, when along came a high pressure salesman from Durham-Draughn Business College in Austin.

He was promoting a wonderful business education (two years), free tuition until graduation, a guarantee of job placement, and free placement with a loving family to work for room and board. What a deal—too good to pass up.

The same salesman sold the same package to parents of my best friend, Louise Wood, so our lives were destined to be closely aligned for life.

On behalf of the school, I will say there were outstanding teachers who took a real interest in the students and the deal of placing with good families was true. Daddy did make one mistake. He wanted to spare me the expense of paying for my tuition after graduation, so somehow he paid it up front. Why was it a mistake? Upon graduation, who got the opportunity to interview for the few jobs that were becoming available? The students who still owed for their education, of course. Paid up people were more or less on their own.

A DREAM NOT REALIZED

We pause to insert a little story that moves fast forward about fifty years to illustrate that mine was not the only dream put on hold. It demonstrates that truly when one door is closed to us, God opens a window of opportunity.

Because of the lack of educational and financial opportunities available to frontier Texans at the beginning of the 20th century, I am convinced the world was denied the wisdom of one who could have been successful in many fields – one of which was the textile industry.

Daddy's first love was family, closely followed by his love of sheep. He would judge the finest of wool either in its raw form or textiles. His dream was that Texas should develop the finest of wool producers and establish a textile industry that could provide textiles equal to or better than that of England and Scotland.

When the oil bust occurred several years ago and Texas was seeking diversity, I was inspired to try to carry on his dream. Gov. Rick Perry was then Secretary of Agriculture. I wrote him a detailed letter outlining such a suggestion. I received a very gracious reply, which, in essence stated, "You have a great idea, good luck in developing it." That was much help, about the same cooperation the government and industry had shown the Wool

Growers Association many years earlier. And we wonder why our textile productions have flown to other countries or why our best manufacturers import their finest cottons from Italy and Switzerland, woolens from England and Scotland, polyesters from China, Japan, India, and so many other places in the world.

For many years I acted as import brokerage account executive handling the Neiman Marcus imports. During one of the famous Neiman Marcus Fortnight promotions, there was some media criticism about the volume of imports, especially regarding men's expensive shoes. About that time there was publicity about shoe manufacturers moving their operations abroad. In a brief conversation with Mr. Stanley, he commented, "If only a U.S. manufacturer would make hand-turned shoes I would buy them. We have a clientele that wants them and I feel we have a right to provide the product."

I suppose my love for textiles, especially wool, comes from my father's gene. Only the lack of funds to support that prevented me from being the very best dressed person around. Even with limited funds, I always preferred to put whatever was available into the purchase of one outfit the fund would cover, rather than two or more cheaper garments. Daddy always supported that and as long as he lived, he always made note of whatever I wore. If it was wool, he was happy. His counsel was. "Daughter, always stay with the naturals, cotton, wool, linen, and silk." He considered man-made fabrics junk. However, such great strides have been made in that field, that I am confident that by today's standards, he might give them limited approval.

I treasure the fact that my father took note of my choice of apparel. That fact was eternally driven home the afternoon before his death at the age of 98. I arrived at his bedside at the hospital. He recognized me and as always, his eyes glowed with happiness to see me. One of his first comments was, "Sister, I sure like your swing bag." He was referring to the soft eel skin leather shoulder bag I was carrying. I said, "I'm glad you like it." As I laid it on the side of his bed, he stroked his hand across it a few times and said the last coherent words I understood: "That's a fine piece of leather and I sure like it."

I no longer carry that old bag, but neither can I discard that fine old leather.

FROM ROUGH CREEK TO AUSTIN TO WASHINGTON

In August of 1938, the business college had arranged for our care-giving families in Austin, so Louise and I boarded a Trailways bus from San Saba to Austin. It never occurred to us to worry about the kind of home we might end up in, but it seemed all the girls the school placed in homes were happy with the arrangements. Generally, we were treated as one of the family. The first family I lived with for almost a year had three children, a little boy, age 4, who loved me, a girl, 9, who loved me and a girl, 12, who hated me because I expected her to abide by rules on the nights I babysat for them.

The second family had a newborn baby I helped care for. I stayed with them until the beginning of my last semester. My eighth baby brother was due in April and Mother was in dire need of help, so I skipped this semester and went home to assist her and especially give a hand with my little sister, Mary Evelyn, Jack, Vernon, and the new arrival, Dewayne.

Louise had been home for the summer and come September mother felt she could again cope so we returned to school to-gether, this time renting a room together and living on cheese and crackers, potted meat, fruit, and all that pastry available from the corner bakery for two to five cents.

As soon as we finished school, both of us found jobs, such as they were. My first job was for a small glass company that did plate glass windows, beautiful mirrors, and replaced windshields. It was a six full days per week at a salary of $7 a week. I went from that to Wallace Engraving for $12 a week.

I have always felt that God provided a special angel for me. This angel places one of her helpers in my path when the need arises. My angel placed at school that opened a window was probably our Commercial Law and Math teacher, Mrs. Finger. She took a special interest in all those struggling country kids seeking opportunities and ways to survive a lingering Depression. She seemed to take a special interest in Louise and me along with about four other students.

Mrs. Finger knew the government was taking a lot of girls to Washington to work in the pre-war emergency. It was necessary to pass a pretty detailed civil service examination. She personally secured the applications to take the examinations, stood over us to see that we filed them, and gave us special training for the tests. Then she was appointed to administer the tests, though she did not get to grade them. Her instructions were that if we passed and were offered an assignment, we should take it. She knew the educational experience would be worth it.

In June 1941, my letter came from the Treasury Department in Washington, suggesting I report by an early July date. I resigned my job, packed my bags, and caught the next bus home to discuss it with my parents. Surprisingly, they were all for it. Daddy gave me money for the train fare from Austin and an extra $100 to tide me over until my first paycheck, plus the security of a promise to send more if I found a need or decided I wanted to come home. Fortunately, I never felt the need and in fact repaid that $100 within a few months.

Just a few days before my letter came, Louise had secured a job with Sears and Roebuck and they had sent her to Waco. I did not have her Waco address, but I reasoned that I would write her parents for her address after I got settled in Washington. Little did I know that she had received a call from the War Department the same day my letter came and that she was traveling by bus the same time I was on the train. We arrived the same morning, both checked into the YWCA, reported our arrival to our respective agencies, and then fell into bed for a long night of much needed sleep. This was on Saturday. Sunday afternoon found both of us in the lobby of the YWCA, frightened, tired, homesick, and wondering how to go about looking for a home. Places to live were already at a premium in Washington.

When it finally dawned on me that the girl across the room in the white blouse and red skirt just like ones Louise had, was really her, I walked across the room and put my arms around her. Two crying young ladies were never as happy to see a loved one as we were. Our troubles seemed to dissolve. We would look for a home together. We secured a list of possible places and instructions on Washington's transportation system and set out looking.

The first place we settled on was a third floor bedroom in one of Washington's big brownstone homes. It was filled with antiques, wide winding stairways and marble baths, but we were not in a position or mood to appreciate the culture surrounding us. We did not like the landlady that kept an eagle eye on all the girls who lived there. Each Sunday everyone left the house for food, sightseeing, or other activities. The landlady positioned herself in a big rocking chair just inside the front door and no one passed without first paying rent for the coming week.

Before long we met a couple of girls we really liked. They were newcomers to the War Department and worked with Louise, Trudy Heffner from San Antonio and a little snowbird from Wisconsin named Virginia. The four of us did some sightseeing together. We were all looking for a better home, so we decided to see if we could find an apartment for four. We were indeed fortunate. A native Washington family had converted their upstairs into an apartment. They said they had been advised against renting to girls, but they were impressed by these Texas girls and decided to take a chance. They never regretted it. After a few months our little snowbird returned home and another of Louise's co-workers, Rita Moss from Arkansas, moved in with us.

For a few weeks, we enjoyed a more or less carefree life of fun. We greatly enhanced our education by visiting all the places of interest we could. We toured the art galleries, the Library of Congress, the Smithsonian, a Franciscan monastery near us, the Skyline drive through the mountains in Virginia during apple harvest time, Mount Vernon, and a memorable trip to New York where we visited Radio City Music Hall and for the first time heard about a wonderful technology that would soon be ours to enjoy – television. They even took some of our party into the studio so the rest of us could view them on closed-circuit TV. Seeing was supposed to be believing. The educational tapes advised that soon we could view live events from any spot in the world. To us, that was unbelievable. We came out of the studio laughing, "Maybe so, but not in our lifetime."

New York had a lot to see, but it was now winter, just a few days before Pearl Harbor. We have complaints today about air quality, but what those cities endured prior to and during the war was something we cannot imagine. A heavy blanket of coal smoke blocked out the sun. On one day while sightseeing, I wore a new beige brushed wool suit. When we returned to the hotel to dress for dinner, my suit looked as if it had been used to clean the flue and my face was black.

We had a party of some 10 co-workers on this trip, most of them from Texas. The evening was to be a visit to one of New York's finest night clubs for dinner and floor show. For the first and only time in my life, I was almost ashamed to be a Texan. About four of the Texas girls decided to put on a show of their own being real "hicks" from Texas and their language and conduct was totally uncalled for. The rest of us disassociated ourselves from them and friendships did not continue after the trip.

This was our last sightseeing trip, because within a couple of weeks the country was at war and all travel was curtailed, and life changed for all of us.

Overnight, life as we knew it had changed. The government offices all converted to three shifts for every 24 hours, and America set its course to do what was necessary to support the all-out war effort. A temporary freeze was put on the sale of all but essential consumer goods while a national rationing program was put into effect.

It is amazing how quickly and efficiently the rationing system was executed. Every man, woman, and child was issued a ration book from which stamps had to be surrendered for a host of consumer goods, particularly in the food chain. Sugar, coffee, and meats were most in demand and the most likely subject to hoarding and black market. Shoe stamps were probably one of the most prized stamps of all. I was caught with only two pairs of shoes and one of those was in need of replacement. Someone in my family donated a shoe stamp for me. Most of the shoe manufacturers converted to production of military footwear as were other products needed for the war effort.

Clothing manufacturers also converted to things military, or were simply short of raw materials because raw cotton and wool were needed elsewhere. Consumer goods such as hose, linens, and household appliances of any kind simply were not available at all or in short supply. One felt as if she had struck a gold mine if she were lucky enough to secure a single pair of nylon hose before the supply was exhausted. After standing in a line three blocks long for such a rare opportunity, it was always a real heartbreaker for the store to come out with the sign, "Sorry, the supply is gone."

Everything from toothpaste tubes (then made of tin) to bacon drippings were saved and donated to the cause. Plastics were still a product of the future and paper for such things as paper bags was limited, so any textiles that had survived the Great Depression was recycled to other uses, such as making our own shopping bags to transport our purchases.

My entry into the Treasury Department was the usual starting place – redeemed currency where tons of currency was returned for cancellation and reissue. It was tattered, dirty money that ended up in the big fiery furnaces after proper verification was made. It is amazing how much was accomplished without such things as electronic helps of any kind. Such things were not to become available until later. There was, however, an efficient work force of old ladies, many who had been doing the routine things since before World War I. They usually knew only one thing and did that well. However, most of them did not have the slightest clue of how the job they did fit in with the responsibility of the worker next door.

I was lucky. I had been there only a few days when I was pushed upstairs to the Bond Department because war bonds were the source of funding for the war effort. Without the helps we now have, it was simply accomplished by orders that came in for thousands of bonds each day. They had to be listed, checked, verified, and assigned to the pool of professional typists (working on the manual typewriters, mostly the dependable Royals or Underwoods). To qualify for this elite pool, the civil service exam needed to reflect that we had successfully passed the congressional test of at least 100 words per minute, error free. Fast forward sixty five years, as I struggle to impute this bit of history into a computer that I fail to understand, I feel a bit of amazement that I accomplished that. My stint behind the typewriter was also short.

The department supervisor assigned me to assist the head typist, whose job was to circulate on the floor of the typing pool where some 300 typists were producing the bonds.

I felt happy and satisfied with what I felt was progress in this wonderful career as a government employee at $1,260 annual salary. That amounted to a cash payment envelope twice a month, each containing two $20 bills, one $10 bill, one $2 bill, plus a new silver half dollar. No taxes, no deductions. I had heard about such a thing as income tax, and I longed for the day when possibly I could qualify to pay such a tax. Little did I know.

AN UNEXPECTED PROMOTION

Maybe the fact that I was a little country girl from Texas who had set her foot in the department had something to do with the next change in my career as a government employee. Late in the spring of 1942, out of the blue, one afternoon my supervisor delivered a message that I was wanted in the personnel office. She had no clue as to why. I had not been to the personnel office since the day I had taken the oath of office and the summons frightened me half to death. To me, it would indicate that there was something wrong, but what?

When I arrived there were two or three people who were wonderful to me and simply wanted to visit with me. They wanted to know where I had been all my life, what I had done, and all about my family. I went home in complete shock. The next day it was the same routine, but different people. The third morning I returned to the bond department, hoping the ordeal of these strange interviews was over, but alas, late in the afternoon the call came to return.

This time, the mystery was lifted and left this young lady in a complete state of shock. The personnel manager said," We know you have been worried about these strange interviews. You have been under consideration for a very important transfer and we can now tell you that you that you have been selected. He then handed me a piece of paper and said, "Monday morning, please report to the security gate, front entrance of the White House, give this piece of paper to the guard, and they will take care of you from there."

Personal long-distance telephone calls were not used during those days, but Western Union was overworked. Confused, frightened, and excited, this young lady went home to suffer anxiety all weekend, stopping on the way to send her parents a telegram which also relieved their mind, because rumors had gotten back to them that some strange officials had been making inquiries about them and their daughter.

At this time, the government was concerned about citizens who may have connections to our foreign ancestors. I suppose that since our family was at least five generations away from our European forefathers, we were deemed to be solid Americans with a loyal history.

Monday morning I put on my only good black dress, hat and gloves and followed the directions given on Friday. The guard at the gate made a telephone call, and within a few minutes, Frank Sanderson, the White House personnel chief, came walking down the driveway. He was a handsome man who stood well over six feet tall and he greeted me as if I were a favorite family member. I loved him from that moment. He took me into the house, directly through the main front entrance, escorted me throughout the downstairs area, including the cabinet room from where President Roosevelt's office was visible, though we did not go there. I was introduced to all the guards, who immediately assigned my nickname, "Miss Texas." Undoubtedly they already knew more about me than I knew about myself, because the secret service had made their report before my assignment had been made.

The East Wing had not been completed. I found I was to be assigned to The Social Office, which was Mrs. Roosevelt's domain. This office was housed in a big room in the basement directly under the front entrance. Mr. Sanderson's office was just around the corner. The office was old, the big wood burning fireplace and big lovely mantel was a central focus. The furniture was antique. My desk was immediately below the window visible at ground level just to the left of the circular drive at the front entrance, so I had a perfect view of the arrival and departure of world leaders and military people from all parts of the world who came calling on President Roosevelt. If they were really important enough for the so-called red carpet to be rolled out, it would be obvious from the personnel that formed the greeting party at the driveway.

From Mrs. Roosevelt, I think this young lady from rural Central Texas first became aware of our needs for civil and human rights as well as the needs of women and children around the world. (See Appendices C and D.)

Mrs. Roosevelt's personal secretary, Dorothy Dow, handled her personal mail, social engagements, appointments, etc. The primary duty of the other staff was to handle the great volume of mail that arrived daily. Mrs. Roosevelt was a lady ahead of her time. She traveled the world over acting as the president's eyes and ears. She made radio talks, wrote magazine articles, and wrote a daily newspaper column, "My Day." She was the nation's first real voice for civil rights, and consequently her activities and her voice brought forth a volume of correspondence never before experienced.

Each letter had to be opened, recorded, and acted upon. Most were referred to various government agencies for action, some referred to Mrs. Roosevelt's secretary for further screening for her possible attention. The letters form the military got top attention. There once appeared a news item that stated all letters from service personnel received an answer and action when warranted. I happened to send a copy of the article to my parents and somehow my letter along with the article made its way into print in the local *San Saba News*. Someone mailed a copy to his son who was with General Patton in North Africa. The home town soldier read it to some of his buddies and a big argument resulted. The general agreement was that it was not true, so to settle the argument the boys decided to write a letter, asking for something perfectly unreasonable, just to see what happened. One of them volunteered to write such a letter.

He wrote a pitiful letter about how hungry he was for something that reminded him of home, and could she please send him a can of pork and beans. The letter made it to her desk. She wrote a personal note across it and forwarded it to the Campbell Company, asking "Can you please see that this boy receives his wish?" What could the wonderful Campbell people do? They dispatched several cases to feed the entire unit.

I was designated file clerk. The White House general correspondence files were kept in long rows of file cabinets that lined about a mile of long dark hallways in the basement of the State Department, just across the alley from the West entrance of the White House. I did not file the correspondence and paperwork, but I learned the codes so I could go and retrieve anything needed. The cold basement was a creepy place. A few big rats resided there, but I was not afraid of them. One became my pet. He would scurry along on top of the files waiting for me to share a candy bar or some nuts I might have in my pocket.

There was an underground cable car that ran from The White House to the Capitol. There was a sweet old man who had been the official courier for this run since the days of President Woodrow Wilson. Now and then he would see me on my way to the file room and ask if I wanted to go with him on a trip to the capitol. The ride on the little cable car was always fun, and I learned many juicy things about the various people we visited on Capitol Hill, because this old man knew everything and everyone.

White House employees had signed a pledge that anything said, read, or heard was confidential. Remember, we were at war and the theory was that, "Even walls have ears" so consequently I never kept notes of some stories I heard. Though I wish I could recall some of the names and events, they have long since faded from memory.

There were only about 145 people attached to The White House staff and I was the youngest. Many had been there since President Wilson. The four years I spent there saw many happy days and our share of tears. The East Wing was completed and the social staff moved to that area, along with new offices for the Secret Service.

A small theater was on the first floor and beneath it all the new air raid shelter. This shelter was a huge steel-like vault. When we had air raid drills, all employees were required to proceed to the safety of that area. When the thick steel doors locked behind us, it was always a scary feeling.

Times were hard for all concerned. There was never enough secure hotel space to care for the many international visitors who came calling, and so very often these guests were invited to stay in the various guest rooms at the White House. This always placed a lot of extra stress on the chief cook, kitchen staff, and household staff as well as Mrs. Roosevelt and the people responsible for the care and comfort of those people. Gossip floated through regarding the stress of a few guests, but none equaled that imposed by Madame Chaing Kai Shek. She came with the general seeking aid in their desperate fight to save Taiwan.

For some reason, she had with her a personal maid, cook, and a few other staff. The cook who insisted access to the kitchen to see the preparation of her meals made Mrs. Nesbit, the person in charge of the kitchen, very unhappy, but the real insult came when Madam went for her afternoon nap. Each time she got out of bed she required fresh sheets before she got in it again. On this occasion, fresh sheets were delivered to her room, but unfortunately some of the linens were old and had been darned after many laundry trips. The White House had been through years of depression prior to the war and money had not been spent on such things as new sheets. The shortage of such things had not concerned Mrs. Roosevelt, and the household staff simply darned linens and made them do.

Madam expressed shock and demanded new sheets. Mrs. Roosevelt was a bit put out, but she took her personal time to try to locate new sheets. None were to be had but an all- out search was initiated by all the stores in Washington. Finally one pair was located in a stock room at Woodard and Lathrop and they delivered them.

LIFE IN WASHINGTON
FOLLOWING DECEMBER 7, 1941

On a quiet Sunday afternoon, December 7, 1941, all fun came to a standstill. Mr. and Mrs. Evans, the wonderful Washington couple who had rented their upstairs to these Texas girls, called us downstairs. He wanted to brief us on what the future probably held.

Mr. Evans was a wheelchair-bound World War I veteran and knew firsthand what war was like. The next weeks and months were filled with adjusted work hours, blackouts, and air raid drills when we shuddered with fear of "Is it real or is it just another drill?"

Entertainment and travel were curtailed. We did have radio and the newspaper published special editions for breaking news. Telephone service was rarely used for personal long distance calls; Western Union was the message system most used and all households trembled with fear when the Western Union boy stood at the door with the familiar yellow message sheet in his hand. Fortunately, most of my messages were happy, like a soldier or sailor friend advising his estimated time of arrival and asking for a date.

There was one sad note from family advising that my parents had received a message that my 19-year old brother in the Navy Air Force was missing on a mission to Japan. A few days later our prayers were answered when we learned that he and only two members of the crew on his plane had been rescued from the waters of the China Sea after three days and nights clinging to life rafts. Eugene was seriously injured and another miracle occurred on the hospital ship bound for the Philippines. A serious infection and blood clots in one leg prompted the doctors to determine that the only possible way to save this sailor's life was to amputate at the hip. He was on the operating table and operation ready to go when to their horror they discovered that the medical supplies did not have any of the clips necessary to clamp off the blood vessels. Without the necessary surgical supplies, the doctor made the decision to simply pump massive doses of penicillin into him every few hours. When they arrived at the hospital the doctors decided that he had survived this far and they would simply continue the penicillin treatment. The suffering was long and painful, but he was able to return to full service. At the end of the war he returned home safely.

He then returned to Kansas where he had met his dream girl while in Navy training there. He married her and they made their home in Kansas and raised a wonderful family there. Eugene always felt God had saved him for something and he dedicated his life to the service of the Master. He was a special son, brother, husband, and father.

My three apartment mates and I got along beautifully in Washington. There was never a cross word between us. We remained close friends. I am the only one remaining and I miss these dear friends, especially around the holidays when we always made special contacts with each other. Each of us had come from different church backgrounds, but we used that as great ecumenical training. Rita, our friend from Arkansas, was a most devout Catholic, having come from a family that produced one brother as a priest and two sisters as nuns. We had a lot to learn from her.

My White House pass would open almost any door, so a couple of my co-workers and I enjoyed a few spots not usually available to everyone. Among them was The National Press Club. Now and then someone special from the national or international scene was scheduled to address the lunch crowd of reporters, journalists, and others. Our pass would allow us in where we could enjoy the same lunch as the noisy crowd and hear the speech and witness the usual upheaval in the Press Club.

As the war progressed, everyone was in turmoil. We four girls were no exception. Louise had met and married a Texas boy in the Navy who was serving on U.S. Destroyers escorting aircraft carriers. Rita decided to join the WAVES (Women's Navy); she liked the snappy blue uniform. Trudy joined the WACS (Women's Army). Her father was a career Army officer.

The Navy personnel serving in the Atlantic got shore leave every now and then when they docked along the East coast.

On one of those occasions, Louise ended up pregnant, which prompted J.L. to rush out on another three-day pass and purchase a house. It was a cute little wartime constructed row house near the historical part of Old Alexandria.

The thought of joining the military did not appeal to me, but my concern for Louise was great so I moved with her into the house in Alexandria, which happened to be just across the highway from a major railroad yard through which it seemed all troop trains passed.

The noise from the trains did not bother me, but those thousands of young sad faces peering from the open windows of those moving trains was a sight that broke many hearts. To this day, if I hear a train's whistle during the night a vision of those faces flash back in memory.

It seems that some memorable events of my life were related to train rides. There was the 1936 all-night ride from San Saba to

Texas Centennial in Dallas—200 miles, 12 hours. There was the exciting 1941 trip from Austin to Washington, D. C., when I was both excited and frightened. I had no idea that I was being transported toward an unbelievable future.

In 1943, my first vacation back to Texas, was at a time when travelling, even with overcrowded trains, it was the norm for ladies to board in dresses, high heels, hats and gloves. Their most important piece of luggage was their hat box.

Dressed as such, this young lady found herself in a crowded coach of servicemen and mothers with crying babies. I was fortunate to find a seat. I had hardly gotten settled when a drunken soldier began unwanted advances. Fortunately, there was a young soldier seated a couple of rows ahead and across the aisle who came to my rescue. In a quiet but forceful way he reminded the young man that he could lose his stripes for such behavior. This young man, on medical leave from Walter Reed Hospital, was on crutches and suffering pain. The banter kept up all night between my protector and the young man who kept returning to try to interrupt my pretended sleep.

Come daylight, my protector stopped by my seat, introduced himself as Willard Morris, and inquired if I had gotten any rest at all. I thanked him for his help and accepted his invitation to accompany him to the dining car for breakfast. When we returned to our coach, the seat beside me was vacant and he moved there for a visit to the point of St. Louis where he changed trains.

It turned out that Willard was from Texas and we were familiar with several places. For instance, he thought he would show me something I would not believe when he pulled a photo from his pocket to indicate a spring of water just below the rim rock of a high mountain. He was shocked when I told him that I not only believed it, I could tell him where it was—the mountain overlooking McCamey, Texas. I further pointed out that there was a pipe going from the spring up over the top. How did

I know that? My father had put it there to pump water over the top for his sheep he had grazing on top of that mountain.

Thus began a friendship that eventually developed into a love that lasted a lifetime. Unfortunately, as often happens in the lives made worse when the stress of war is involved, mistakes are made, misunderstandings arise and plans for the future differ, resulting in two people who take different routes. The rest of the story lies later, after some of the trails through the valley of life are told.

AN UNFORGETABLE
CHRISTMAS RECEPTION

On Christmas Eve, 1944, the White House staff was invited to the president's office for personal greetings from President Roosevelt, to receive our Christmas gifts, and mingle with the rest of the staff.

One of the girls from my office and I arrived at the Cabinet room a little early. General Watson, the president's chief of staff, was alone in the room and he came to greet us, put an arm around each of us and said, "Come on girls, I am going to take you in for a private meeting with the president."

Surprised, we insisted that we would wait for the reception to begin, but by that time he had pulled us into the view of the open door of the oval office and the president saw us and called out, "Oh, come on in girls, I have yet to bite anyone." We were escorted to President Roosevelt's desk where he held each of us by the hand and chatted for a couple of minutes. Because of my excitement, I never could remember exactly what he asked, or my answer. The warm glow of that moment never left.

The staff gift this Christmas was a limited edition of a scroll of President Roosevelt's D-Day Prayer. There were only 145 of these commissioned, and it is one of the most valuable items in my estate.

The following Christmas, President Truman's gift was an autographed companion scroll of his prayer commemorating the end of the war.

Not long after this Christmas reception, President Roosevelt left to meet with Winston Churchill and Josef Stalin at the historic Yalta conference. The war was at a crucial stage and continued to take its heavy toll on the nation and it was most evident in the failing health of the president. The voyage was aboard a warship, in bitter cold, rough seas, heavy security, and total secrecy. General Watson took ill and died on the return voyage and President Roosevelt was surely weakened.

A DINNER PARTY TO BE REMEMBERED

While President Roosevelt was away on the Yalta trip, things were strangely quiet and tense in the White House. Concerns were high.

Perhaps to relieve her anxiety as much as anything, Mrs. Roosevelt decided this was a good time to honor the White House staff who faithfully shared her stress. She announced a dinner party for us. Invitations were issued in the traditional White House manner. My guest ticket was cancelled and returned to me as a souvenir. It is another of my treasures.

On the designated evening, we gathered in the State Dining Room. Tables for about six were elegantly set with the fine china and silver. During the evening, Mrs. Roosevelt made it a point to sit for a few minutes at each table and chat with each of us. She had a special talent for making those around her comfortable.

In our excitement of this special dinner, I doubt that any of us could remember what was on the menu.

SHALL WE HAVE A FOURTH-TERM PRSIDENT?

(See Appendix E.)

Presidential campaigns had never impacted my life. I remember our parents and friends complaining bitterly about the Hoover period when the Great Depression descended upon the nation, and the excitement when President Roosevelt came to the oval office in 1933 and began his radio addresses to try to calm the nation's fears.

There were many who opposed all the quick reforms that were put in place to try to pull the nation from the quagmire, but in the end hope returned. Great strides were made in the improvement of the transportation system by the construction of roads, bridges, and rail systems.

Electrification came to rural America years ahead of schedule. Scientific and medical research programs were begun, some of which resulted in life-saving medicine that served well during the war. The most notable of these was penicillin.

Some government programs were put in place, some good, some bad, but the one that remains as a lifesaver today was the

Social Security program. Even with its problems, can we imagine what life today would be like without it?

The president's cry for us to prepare for our defense was fought by the isolationists in our Congress. There were those then, as today, who felt we should simply ignore the dangers involving others, not spend money or manpower preparing for our defense, until war came our way at the unexpected attack on Pearl Harbor. We were caught napping and unprepared.

Now at the height of another presidential election year the question arose, "Do we change commander-in-chief during the heat of battle?"

The party in power decided, "No" and nominated President Roosevelt for a fourth term. To campaign at this critical time took time and strength that he could hardly afford, but he handily won the fourth term.

The inauguration was scaled back to be brief and without the pageantry usually associated with inaugurations. Instead of holding it at the Capitol with a parade it was conducted from the South Portico of the White House which overlooks the beautiful grounds. This happened on a cold January day with several inches of snow on the ground. To witness this historical event, there was a limited crowd of invited guests, government and military officials, special guests, and the White House staff.

I was one of those who stood in the cold that day, but the thrill of the occasion kept the cold at bay and the protective galoshes kept our precious shoes dry and feet warm.

A LIMO RIDE THAT CREATED A LIFETIME OF MEMORIES

During this lull of activity in the West Wing of the White House, it seemed a good time to catch up on other small details. One was to see that those on the staff who were signed up to be regular blood donors were given time to go make their gifts of blood.

I was one of the few young enough and healthy enough to be on that list. On a warm afternoon, Mr. Sanderson called me to come over to the personnel office and someone would drive me to the Red Cross which was located on the Capitol grounds.

Upon arrival, Mr. Sanderson decided he wanted to take a break and he would take me himself. When we stepped out into the driveway, there sat the president's limo with Peppi, his chauffer, sitting beside it looking perfectly bored. Mr. Sanderson said, "Oh, what the heck, let's go in style." So, he ushered me into the back seat of that limo and they delivered me to the Red Cross building, leaving me with instructions to simply go on home after my gift of blood.

After giving my pint of blood (it was the sixth overall I had given), I walked with several other donors to the bus stop beside the circular drive in front of the Capitol building.

Suddenly, I wondered why I had brought with me a book I was reading because it seemed so heavy and then I blacked out and fell off the curb onto the gravel-covered street just as some senator's black limo came around the drive. Apparently he was a good person, because when I came to, I was stretched out on the front seat of his limo with nurses trying to wake me up. They returned me to the blood center in a wheelchair, gave me something to drink and eat and wanted to notify someone to come get me. I had to show my White House pass to prove I wanted the White House to come get me.

Within a very few minutes, both Mr. Sanderson and Peppi were standing in the doorway. They laughed out loud at the sight of me. They were still driving the president's limo so they delivered me home. I have no idea of the impression that limo with the president's seal and flags flying made as it pulled into the drive of that modest little row house in Alexandria, but I do know that the girl who disembarked with a bloody dress, skinned elbows and knees made quite a sight and a story that circulated the rounds of the entire White House staff.

A NATION GRIEVES AND FACES
A NEW CHALLENGE

On April 12, 1945, the nation went into shocked grief at the sudden death of President Roosevelt. History has well recorded details of those sad events. It is hard to describe the grief of the staff as all activities had to continue. Flowers banked all the halls from floor to ceiling. A private funeral was held in the East Room for staff, invited officials, and guests.

I can only add to recorded history my memory of the great sadness that fell over the White House staff along with the entire nation; the fear of the unknown as we looked to the leadership of a new president who seemed to be virtually unknown to the public, and the avalanche of mail that descended upon those of us designated to open, read, and act upon it.

A frightened nation did not know what to expect from its new leader, Harry Truman. Little was known about this quiet little man from Missouri, but history has shown that he was the leader we needed at that hour. God provides.

The onslaught of mail was unbelievable. Each piece had to be opened and recorded without electronic helps. Most letters contained money, dollars but mostly small change, especially dimes, but it was enough to fund the final research for the cure of the dread polio which had crippled the president as a young man.

When I left the White House the office presented me with the common, government- issued letter opener that had slit so many thousand letters. It is a cherished keepsake.

Once all that mail was handled, the White House settled into a real period of general quiet. All social occasions were curtailed for a year. Mrs. Truman did not make speeches, write a column, or cause controversy with outside activities. Consequently, she was not the target for the correspondence that results from such activities. The few of us left in the Social Office looked forward to Friday afternoons because President Truman usually came to the theater which was just down the stairs from our office to review the newsreels that had been returned from various parts of the world. Remember this was before TV. Quite often one of the local theaters would send over a great movie that was to be shown for the president to enjoy. He always asked that those girls with nothing to do join him. Mrs. Truman and Margaret usually accompanied him, but he claimed that he wanted company behind him when he watched a movie.

After the war ended, everyone seemed to be leaving Washington so it was not hard for me to make a decision to look beyond.

Louise's Navy husband returned from four years of horrible war experiences. He had survived the sinking of two destroyers on which he served. They were ready to sell the little house in Alexandria, take the new baby, and return to the peace of Texas.

To see my best friend take the baby I loved as if it were my own really hurt, but I was rejoicing for Louise and J.L. Temples.

Another friend had been sharing the house in Alexandria with Louise and me, and we went searching for a place to move.

Housing was in shorter supply at the end of the war than it had been at the beginning.

A new housing development was being constructed on a mountainside near Arlington cemetery and we took a unit with the understanding that by the time we moved into it, bus services would be at the end of our street. It did not happen and the house was terrible. The units were built into the side of the mountain. I hope the city of Arlington has long since removed this development and returned that mountain to the wild. The bottom street was nearest so we entered from the back, up 30 steps and across a small yard. Then we entered through the basement where resided the coal-fired furnace and that dirty stack of cheap black coal (the only kind available at the time).

We walked up five steps to a small kitchen, dining and living area, up another flight of steps to bedroom and bath, and up another stairway to a second bedroom and bath. The window of this top bedroom was level with the street above the house.

Each night the fire would die in that furnace and at 5:00 a.m. I found myself trucking down to that cold basement and struggling to bring enough life back into the fire to half- way warm the house.

In August I had suffered a severe throat infection that had kept me out of work for 30 days. The doctor stated my future health demanded that my tonsils be removed. I entered the hospital in October for that procedure, shortly after our move into the Arlington house.

When I was released from the hospital several days later, the temperature was in the 20s and snow was falling. The bus stop was six blocks away. Those long cold walks to the bus, having to stand up on a crowded bus for the trip into Washington, plus the struggles of that coal-fired furnace kept me half sick all winter, so come spring I was depressed and ready to come back to Texas.

In February, I made a trip home by way of Dallas, made two interviews, was accepted at the Federal Deposit Insurance Corporation, and when I returned to Washington, the request for my transfer was waiting for me.

In April, some of that dirty snow from October still lay around, so my joy knew no bounds when I arrived in Dallas on April 22, 1946, to beautiful warm weather and roses in full bloom.

Dallas also had a severe housing shortage. Someone suggested I place my own ad in the paper seeking shelter. I did and left my hotel telephone number. Many people responded to the ad, but a great many of them were in undesirable locations. I did not know the city or the streets, but since taxi fare was cheap, I simply used a taxi to take me around. Most often when we found the address I did not even get out of the taxi.

On the second day I was lucky. A lovely elderly couple with a neat home near White Rock Lake was happy to take me in. The streetcar to downtown was handy.

The FDIC office was in the Federal Reserve Bank building. There were many places to eat breakfast, lunch, and dinner downtown at very reasonable prices. A drugstore at the corner of Elm or Main and Akard served a wonderful breakfast for 35 cents.

I loved the job at FDIC, but soon faced the fact that the greatest discrimination against women in employment was our federal government.

Because of a vacancy in the office, I was assigned the task of chief clerk, which warranted a salary of more than twice what I was being paid. The supervising examiner of the Dallas office begged Washington to certify me to that job, but no; it was classified as a man's job with a rating of at least assistant bank examiner. Women could not train to become bank examiners either.

Had I known that down the road things would change, I may have stuck it out and remained a federal employee. In a way, that was probably luck, because I would have missed two great opportunities in employment for expanding my knowledge plus the satisfaction of feeling I had a small part in the development of two industries that have greatly impacted our city.

The mother of a young lady I worked with at FDIC worked at Dallas Power and Light and was a close friend of Mrs. Florence Lowe, secretary to the president of DP&L.

One Sunday afternoon in 1948, this friend invited me to a party where both those ladies were present. After some conversation with Mrs. Lowe, she decided I must go to work for her son's new air conditioning company.

Shortly after the war, Jack Lowe, Sr. had established Texas Distributors, Inc., and his goal was to cool Dallas. Very few small businesses had central refrigerated air and only 40 residents in Dallas had central systems and those were commercial units.

Mr. Lowe started begging manufacturers to design smaller units for residential application. All laughed at him, claiming there would be no market for them. Those east coast manufacturers had never spent a summer in Texas.

Texas Distributors was the distributor for General Electric gas fired furnaces, so finally GE agreed to come up with a few air conditioning units.

Fortunately, this happened about the time Dallas entered the housing construction. Fox and Jacobs, a new builder, was the first to try this experience. They were to build a development near Casa Linda. General Electric assisted with the expense of massive advertising in conjunction with the opening of the first model house. The idea created a traffic jam and media excitement. It was news in every builder- and construction-type publication.

Manufacturers took notice and other builders put housing plans on hold to make plans for central air. Suddenly, we had accomplished the goal. It made cooling a necessity, not just a luxury.

I had worked hard trying to succeed with advertising and sales promotion. The concept that men ruled in the business world still prevailed.

General Electric sponsored an advertising contest, offering a prize to the advertising manager who designed the best advertising campaign for central air. My proposed concept, which TDI used, won the contest and then GE did not know what to do about the prize. It had been advertised to be a Hart, Schaffner Marx suit to be furnished by James K. Wilson men's store if won in our area. The question was settled with a check for me to go choose my own outfit.

To see an industry born, thrive, and become a shining example of success gave me a great sense of satisfaction and I shall cherish the memory of the twenty years association with the original players.

Because of some personal burdens in 1968, it seemed I needed to make a change. A friend who had an employment office downtown scheduled an appointment with Joe Sekin, owner of a fairly new custom house brokerage firm. We spent about five hours in that initial interview where I probably asked more questions than I received, but from it I gained confidence that this was a person I could trust. Forty years later I was proven right.

My initial concern was that I would not be held back from anything I was capable of because I was a woman, and that my compensation would be fair.

It was not easy to go from a business I knew so well to one I knew nothing about— International Business, with rules and regulations of U.S. Customs, U. S. traffic schedules, and all other kinds of things involving international business and transportation. For a few weeks, I wondered what I had done to myself, but Mr. Sekin was a wonderful and patient teacher, the local U.S. Customs personnel were most helpful in my ongoing education, and customers assigned to me were loyal and helpful. One never learns it all, and rules keep changing, but it was and still is a challenging experience.

In 1984 all of us who worked for Mr. Sekin were heartbroken when he sold the company.

The new owner immediately made many changes. He interviewed each employee, let a few go, chose a few to stay and lifted the titles of all of us who held positions of responsibility. I needed my job, so I did not grieve for the loss of the title as vice president since no salary cut came with it.

When Mr. Sekin had advanced my position to that of vice president a few years earlier, he had given me a few shares of stock. The stock had little value at the time, so I placed the certificates in the bottom of my lingerie drawer and had forgotten them.

The new owner wanted to secure all the outstanding stock held by a few of the employees. A few sold their stock to him at low prices. Every few months he would make me a new offer for my shares. A few times I was tempted, but for some reason I resisted. I was not suffering financially on my salary and felt if they were that valuable to him they might be worth keeping.

The goal of the new management was to take the company public, which was accomplished. Just before the transaction to go public was completed, he made one last offer for my stock, explaining that once the transfer was made, the sale would be frozen for some five years. Some of us took the risk and kept the stock. In 1995 I sold the stock for about four times the amount offered on the day it was frozen.

Unfortunately, because of my ignorance in the art of investment, capital gains and other options that may have been available to me, the IRS assessed capital gains to the tune of about five years' salary. I relied on advice of the brokerage firm and the CPA I was using. Nevertheless that bequeath of stock has offered some degree of comfort I would never have otherwise enjoyed, and for that I am forever grateful for an employer who kept his word.

After I retired in 1995, I stayed home for a few months and involved myself with new grandchildren, church and civic affairs, but I missed being involved.

The Sekin family came to my rescue by suggesting I return as a part-time employee of their son's new brokerage business. This wonderful association kept me somewhat involved in the ever-changing rules and regulations of international trade for another 10 years.

In December 2007, age 89, with the creeping reminder that impaired vision was becoming a problem that made me a hazard to both myself and others on the highway, I was reminded that it was again time to retire.

WHERE HE LEADS ME
I WILL FOLLOW

When this young lady arrived in Dallas on April 22, 1946, suffering from the stress of coping with war-related problems of survival, coupled with lingering effects of a serious illness in the summer and fall of 1945, followed by that last hard winter in Washington, she found herself much in need of spiritual comfort and self assurance. She realized that the decision to give up a cherished position as a permanent member of the White House staff and relocate to a strange city was in accordance with God's plan for her life.

With a rear view perception, I feel it was God's will. Had I remained in Washington, I may have still been there during the Nixon period when some innocent staff members suffered political harassment. There were times during this sad time when I breathed a prayer of thanksgiving, saying, "But for the grace of God, that could have been me." Had I continued in the filing and documentation process and knowing my level of loyalty and sense for following instructions, I feel sure that had a supervisor handed me a stack of documents with instructions to destroy them, into the fiery furnace they would have gone.

Has life been a walk down a path of honeysuckle and roses? No, but it has led along a sparkly stream that reflects back the heavenly hues of the rainbow that obscures the briars and brambles and lights the spirit of eternal hope. My first priority was to find a church home. I visited a couple of churches in the East Dallas area but felt I needed more. I inquired as to whether there was a downtown Methodist church. Fortunately, I was referred to First United Methodist Church. On a cool October morning I arrived via street car and found myself seated in a beautiful sanctuary among a sea of strangers. It just so happened that this was the first sermon from that pulpit for a young new pastor named Robert E. (Bob) Goodrich. His congregation represented the heart of Dallas who had given their all to fill leadership positions in Dallas and help the church survive the Great Depression and World War II.

A stranger this sad young lady did not remain. On this very morning she sat beside the beautiful Mary Lou Branson. She reached out to me, introduced herself and some others in the area and together they recruited me to consider their Sunday School class. They even made arrangements for someone to pick me up the following Sunday to attend the class annual sunrise breakfast at beautiful Flagpole Hill. This was a large class of young, active, and enthusiastic people whose teacher, Mr. M.J. Norrel, gave lessons that had an impact for life. To this day, I can recall his beautiful ringing voice as it vibrated through the entire downstairs of the church as he imparted those unforgettable lessons.

The next eight years of my life were happy and carefree, actively employed in challenging work and totally immersed in church activities. I served in many offices of the Sunday School class including president two or three times, but my greatest focus was the women's work. My interest was to help improve the status of women in the realms of education, social and fields of employment. This entry was through the Wesleyan Service Guild, the business and professional woman's arm of what is now named United Methodist Women. In that organization I served in various local, district and conference positions and it was there that

I forged friendships I shall never forget. They have all preceded me to heaven, but at least I know that these will greet me with open arms some day: Mary Lou Branson, Mary Lou Stewart, Martha Ferguson, Madge Harris, Minnealeatha Prater, Winnie Ball, Lola Bass Newman, Catherine Reeves, and oh so many more.

I had no thought of ever changing directions from where I was headed— a single, gainfully employed woman, older sister to my eight brothers and one lovely sister and auntie to all those cute little nieces and nephews that were rapidly filling our parents' home on holidays and summer vacations. I think Mother thought I was wasting my life.

In the summer of 1954, after years with no communication, my phone rang and the familiar voice of Willard Morris came through with all the charm I suppose I had never forgotten. Result: our marriage December 31, 1954, his relocation to Dallas, and my life's taking a completely new focus.

A baby on the way: could anyone with her future all mapped out cope? God in His infinite wisdom can help one do so. A son, George, who arrived at my age of 35, and a daughter, Mollie-B, at age 38 completely changed my life and provided the most satisfaction.

Unfortunately, when George was only a year old, Willard had to face three bouts of pneumonia in a year, complicated by addition to cigarettes, which resulted in life-threatening emphysema, the ravages of which brought about five years of extreme stress, worry and financial strain. Faith, the power of prayer, and the rallying of faithful friends saw us through.

My husband's health had declined steadily, and the doctors had prepared us both that death was certain and would come soon, possibly without warning, which doubly increased the burden of stress. My husband feared for the children's sake should such an emergency occur while he was alone with them, so a dear and loving black friend was employed to stay at home with the family while I worked long hours.

I shall always give thanks for my husband's help with the children these last few precious months. George had just entered the teen years, and my husband was concerned about me for the coming years. He worked hard to instill in our son a sense of responsibility and respect for me, his mother, and women in general. I can honestly say that neither of my children ever caused any worry. They have been God's greatest gift. George and his family have moved several times, settling in Bowling Green, Kentucky, and Mollie-B now (2009) lives with me in Dallas.

If anyone should ask what I feel my greatest accomplishment in life has been, without hesitation it would have to be the roles of mother and grandmother.

Professional life has been a source of personal satisfaction and growth and to a limited degree an opportunity to serve others. Motherhood and playing the game as a care-giving grandmother has fulfilled the ultimate desire of the heart.

To underline our unfailing belief in the power of prayer and guardian angels, we record two stories that forever impacted our life.

To illustrate the power of prayer is one we call "The Story of the Little Black Dress." October 1969 brought the death of my husband and father of a son age 13 and daughter, 9. Our sweet little black friend, Johnny Bell, had returned to her life of caring for others. She had been my life saver as she cared for my family while I worked long hours.

With the help of loyal and faithful friends from First Methodist Church and particularly from the Wesleyan Service Guild, we set about to rebuild our lives and pay the debts. This wonderful group, determined to see that I became active and stayed involved, somehow convinced me to serve as president. It seemed I served in all capacities of the local group, followed by serving as District Secretary and a spot on the North Texas Conference Board. Along the way, I served on the Board of Church Women United. During my tenure as conference officer, some committee chose me to be featured as Christian Woman of the Year for an article in *The World Outlook* magazine (January 1955).

At this period in history, the early 1970s, the Woman's Society of Christian Service (now United Methodist Women) and the Wesleyan Service Guild held a joint spring banquet at which the men of the church were special guests.

As president of the guild, which was to hostess this banquet, I had invited our then very popular District Attorney, Henry Wade, to be the speaker. To preside at this upcoming occasion I felt it imperative that I have a new dress since I had not indulged in such expense for far too long. I set aside a special savings for the expenditure. Come January, we had saved $100 for this project. We hoped by March to add enough for a new pair of shoes.

In the early 1970s Dallas was subject to at least one terrible ice storm each January and this year was no exception. The sleet was falling, the night was bitter when the telephone rang. It was Parkland Hospital. The nurse on the line wanted to tell me that they had a little patient named Johnny Bell in emergency. They were preparing to take her to surgery to amputate one leg due to a horrible infection. I offered to go but the nurse insisted I not come out in the night because Johnny would be out of it all night and would not know I was there.

To the hospital's credit, I shall always remain amazed and grateful for the care and compassion shown to both the patient, a ward of the county, and to me. The nurse called me three times during the night to advise about her progress.

Later a case worker was assigned to Johnny, and working with her we were able to establish Medicare benefits and her Social Security which was way past due. The case worker even arranged for her move to a new high rise apartment that had some apartments for the handicapped.

Johnny Bell was ready to go home, but the hospital said they could not release her until she had a wheelchair. Medicare did not furnish one. The Red Cross, Salvation Army, and anyone else I could contact were trying to help, but no one had a chair. What to do? Asking God for help seemed to be the only way, so we prayed that God would give us the grace to preside in that tired old dress, and the children and I took the $100, went to a hospital supply house that had agreed to sell us a like-new wheelchair for $100. We took the chair to Parkland to secure Johnny Bell and take her to her new home. Johnny had always been the life of the party and during her long stay at the hospital had made friends with everyone on her wing of the hospital, so she got in that chair and scooted the entire length of the wing calling for all her friends to come see what her friends had brought her.

Sunday morning the children and I were in our usual spot in church, and sitting behind us was a retired friend from the guild. Her lifelong employment had been personal secretary to the president of the Dallas Cotton Exchange. His widow, a world traveler and compulsive shopper, had continued to care for Ruth. On her return from trips she often delivered clothing she had purchased and then discovered she neither needed nor wanted them. She would deliver them to Ruth, an excellent seamstress, to redo for a couple of nieces she was helping put through college.

Shortly after we got home this Sunday, the phone rang and it was Ruth. She said this traveling friend had delivered some new dresses to her the day before and she said that she felt they were my size. She hoped I would not feel hurt if she offered them. Hurt? The children and I could hardly wait to get to her house. Sure enough there was a lovely black designer dress and two lovely professional ones, the price tag still attached, and all a perfect fit.

That little black dress will reside in the bottom of my old cedar chest along with a copy of this story. Perhaps at some future date a great granddaughter will be reminded that a grandmother relied on prayer and that God truly provides.

GUARDIAN ANGELS ARE REAL

Literature, art, and dreams have always portrayed the vision of angels. I am sure the devil has his messengers out seeking the hearts and souls of each of us, but I also happen to believe that God assigns a guardian angel for his children of faith. One dramatic event lives vividly in my heart as proof. I shall record it as "A Miracle on Highway 67."

Riding in a new Dodge sedan, before seat belts and child protective devices, my son three and a half, my daughter, five months, and a friend's child the same age as my son were with me on a trip to my parents in Central Texas. Between Glen Rose and Hico, in a hilly and curved road area, following a car ahead at a safe distance, I was aware of no problems. Suddenly the people in the car ahead realized they had just passed a desired turn off to a country road, put on brakes and started backing up. No problem, I simply increased speed to go around them when suddenly and to my horror there appeared over the hill a car coming at a high speed. I was in their path, headed for a head-on crash.

To correct back into my lane would put me into the collision with the car backing up and there was a country mailbox on a heavy post on the right shoulder. I know I did not have the time or ability to think about the proper reaction, so I am fully confident that my angel put me to sleep, took the wheel, and flew us to safety.

I will never know whether I simply blacked out, or whether my angel put me into a trance of some kind. I do know that I was brought back by a sweet little voice behind me with a question, "Mommy, did we nearly wreck?" "Yes, darling, we did and God saved us," I said, and I burst out crying harder than ever before in my life, even as we gave praise and thanks. Nothing short of a miracle could have moved that car across a rough bar ditch some 50 feet wide, perfectly aligned it beside the ranch fence on top of an embankment some three or four feet high, and yet two small children in the back and a baby perfectly sleeping on the seat beside me were not in the least disturbed. It was several minutes before I had the strength to get out of the car to inspect for any damage. There was none, so we safely guided the car off that embankment, across the bar ditch and back on the highway to complete our journey. We described this miracle to my parents and they joined me in again giving thanks.

CONCLUSION

The world we know today is much different from that which I knew as a child. Television shows us the world. Telephone, fax, and e-mail have brought instant communications to far reaches of the world. We have faster and better transportation, though still dangerous. We have rural electricity, refrigeration, air conditioning, fast food, frozen dinners, and oh so much more.

These were all wonderful changes, but ones that created life in the fast lane that has challenged the mission of the church in many ways. We still have the poor, the homeless, and those much in the need of God's grace.

Now, over sixty years after my service in Washington, my scope of activities has not been the level of service I would like, but my interest in promoting the welfare of women and children has not diminished.

Now as we settle into what is considered the wonderful autumn years, we are determined not to fear the future, but rather that we may be granted the peace to understand God's plan for bringing our life to its ultimate goal by letting us see the stumbles in our steps, the blips in our memory, the flashes of blindness that sweep across the page and miss words in conversation surrounding us not as handicaps to fear, but rather the gentle preparation for bringing us to that goal with peace and understanding, secure in the knowledge that He will bring us safely home and return to comfort and assure those left behind.

I am confident my faithful angel will remain by my side to gently put me to sleep and maneuver me across the divide and then return to comfort my loved ones.

I would like to review my life as that of a beautiful plant that bursts forth in the spring, grows, produces, accomplishes its mission and come fall, the seeds mature, the leaves take on beautiful colors, fall to the earth and the cycle of life begins anew.

APPENDIX A: THE WHITE HOUSE

(Due to age, this document is copied rather than being scanned. Any changes from the original are placed in parentheses.)

The cornerstone of the White House was laid October 13, 1792, and the building was completed in 1800. The land was purchased from David Burns. The architect of the White House was James Hoban, who was born in Dublin, Ireland.

The White House was the first public building built in Washington. There are 16 ½ acres of land in the White House grounds.

The White House is built of a buff-colored sandstone from Aqua Creek in Virginia. (A) fire in 1814 burned and blackened the stone so much that it had to be painted white.

The south portico was built in 1823; the north portico in 1829. Gas lights were first installed in 1848. A heating and ventilating system was installed in 1853. The East Terrace was removed in 1870 and was re-built in 1903-03. The length of the White House is 460 feet.

The first cook stove and bathtub (were) installed in 1857. The first electric lights were installed by President Benjamin Harrison in 1888. The first electric refrigerating plant was installed in 1926.

The East Room is 80 feet long and 40 feet wide and 22 feet from floor to ceiling. It was opened to the public for the first time when President Monroe's daughter was married to the Governor of New York in 1820.

In 1895 there were 27 guards at the White House and now (about 1942) the number is a little less than 150. The White House police force was inaugurated in 1922.

The first letter received in the East Room by a president was by President John Adams.

The three chandeliers in the East Room contain 18,900 pieces of cut glass.

The White House was first called the "President's Palace" and then changed to the "President's House."

The first New Year's reception was given January 1, 1801, by President and Mrs. John Adams.

The carved marble mantels in the red and green parlors were removed from the State Dining Room by Theodore Roosevelt. They were carved in London, England. The gilt bronze and marble clock in the Blue Room was a gift from Napoleon to Lafayette who presented it to President George Washington. It is still running and keeps good time. The tall mahogany grandfather clock in the second floor hall was brought by President Arthur.

The British set the White House afire August 24, 1814. The White House was restored by President Theodore Roosevelt in 1902. The architects were McKim, Mead, and White.

The White House executive offices were remodeled and enlarged by President Franklin D. Roosevelt in 1934. Lorenzo S. Winslow was the architect.

The White House kitchens were changed from gas to all electric; the ground floor was remodeled and the carpenter, paint, shops, and store rooms installed under the north lawn in 1936. Lorenzo S. Winslow was the architect. The old electric wiring was removed and new electrical work installed in the White House in 1936-37.

The White House swimming pool was built a few months after Franklin D. Roosevelt was inaugurated in 1933. Lorenzo S. Winslow was the architect.

The White House grounds were laid out by Landscape Architect Downing about 1850. There are many trees (on) the grounds that were planted by different (p)residents from John Adams' time.

The East Wing was started after war was declared in 1941. It contains a concrete bomb proof shelter, air raid signal room, and rooms for the White House Police Force. A (m)otion picture room was also installed. The architect was Lorenzo S. Winslow.

A new road was installed in the South Grounds in 1937 when the Old Carriage roads were removed.

APPENDIX B: DISCRIPTION OF THE WHITE HOUSE GROUNDS

(On) the grounds of the White House, which one hundred years ago was called "The President's Park," there are American Elm trees planted by presidents John Quincy Adams, Rutherford Hays, Woodrow Wilson, and Herbert Hoover; oaks planted by Benjamin Harrison, William McKinley, Herbert Hoover, and Theodore Roosevelt; a Japanese Maple by Grover Cleveland; a white birch by Calvin Coolidge, and two American Lindens by Franklin D. Roosevelt in commemoration of the visit of the King and Queen of England in 1939. Perhaps the best known trees are two Southern Magnolia grandifloras brought from the Hermitage and planted on the southwest corner of the White House by Andrew Jackson. There are also numerous trees planted by all the presidents' wives.

Throughout the grounds there are many well known native trees and also many trees from distant lands such as the deodar, which is a beautiful half cedar half pine tree from India and the Royal Paulownia from Siam, which has gorgeous blue iris-like blossoms.

North of the West Terraces there are five rare and beautiful fern leafed beech trees. Other rare trees are the Chinese

Goldenrain tree, Chinese Scholar tree, Mainenhair tree, Japanese Hope trees, Atlas Cedar and Chestnut oaks. There are two groups of Bald Cypress which are unusual in this vicinity.

South of the Executive Offices there is a mint bed that has been here for over fifty years.

Under the Jackson Magnolias many first ladies had afternoon tea, and in pleasant weather President Franklin Roosevelt and his friends had lunch there.

After the East Wing was completed in 1942, the grounds adjacent were landscaped with large specimens of boxwood and at each end of the building, groups of Pink Magnolias, rhododendrons, firehorne and flowering crabapple trees were set out. White dogwood, white and rose azaleas, and rare, fragrant star magnolia were also planted.

The rather informal East Garden between the White House and the East Wing has numerous perennial flower borders so arranged as to have plants in bloom from early spring until December. There is a marble bordered reflecting pool in this garden where water lilies of various colors are in bloom during the summer. Near the East Wing there is a large rose bed planted with all the newer roses of every shape and color.

The West Garden between the White House and the president's office and cabinet room, is a formal garden with boxwood bordered rose beds, and walks. The principal rose planted here is the red radiance as this rose continually blooms from early spring until late autumn. There is one large bed near the president's office, of a beautiful salmon and orange rose called Grand Duchess Charlotte of Luxemburg.

At the southern end of the grounds there are several large beds of varied colored roses.

Plans have been made for developing and planting the gardens and grounds in an artistic and modern manner in keeping with the White House.

APPENDIX C: MRS. ROOSEVELT'S FIRST RADIO ADDRESS

(Date: December 9, 1932. Any changes to the original
are in parentheses.)

It is almost impossible to compare the girl of today with the girl of thirty or forty years ago, not because the girls have changed, in spite of what some of my contemporaries think, but because the world we live in has changed so greatly. When I was eighteen, automobiles existed but they were still rare enough to cause the horse I was (riding), in the quiet country spot on the Hudson, where we spent our summers, to leap over a stone wall taking the two-wheeled cart and its occupants with him! It was all so sudden that I came to see the horse grazing in the field, while we picked ourselves up off the ground and saw a disappearing car in the dim distance! Now my children's horses take an automobile as a matter of course and even pay little attention to an (airplane) flying overhead!

It isn't, however, so much the fact that we have all these new inventions, such as cars and (airplanes), telephones, radios, electric light and movies, but the change which they have wrought in the speed of life. We can know and see so many people, we can do so much more in a day, even if we have to work in our own homes, it is so much easier and quicker to do if you can afford to use modern inventions that the girl of parents who are moderately well off, even the girl on a farm, may do things that would have been out of the question when I was young.

My generation's problems fundamentally were much the same as are the problems facing the girl today. We had home responsibilities and we accepted them or shirked them much as does the girl of today, but our chief preoccupation was getting to know people, girls and boys, and making friends. We were having as good a time as we could have, doing some work and incidentally finding out what in this world, which at that time we felt largely was created for us alone, really was of interest to us and vital enough to become a permanent part of the life which we were planning for ourselves. Isn't this about the same thing which the girl of today is doing? Only instead of horses and buggies, she has a roadster or a sedan; instead of going to one place in a day and seeing a few people, she can go to four or five and see an almost unlimited number, instead of being tied down many hours by work at home or in a shop, she has more hours to play, instead of seeing her friends at home or in a neighbor's house, she goes to a movie in a nearby town, to people's houses whom her parents do not know, or to a dance hall away from home. There is greater opportunity to develop, perhaps, and with wise parents the girl of today is perhaps earlier able to judge between (worthwhile) people and undesirable ones. She is better able to take care of herself because her experience is greater, but on the other hand, there are more temptations and they come courting her more frequently.

She is away from parental supervision much younger than was the case in my youth. Unless the parents have been wise and trained her young to judge for herself and decide between right and wrong, she is apt to have some rather bitter experiences. Also she will have some disillusionments about people for youth is likely to clothe the object of its enthusiasm with the virtues which a fertile imagination can produce, and it is a sad awakening to find that human nature is far from perfect, and that people cannot always be trusted.

In my youth all of us saw wine on the table in our homes and many of us saw a good bit of excessive drinking, but very few girls, whether in high school or private school or college drank anything beyond a glass of wine at home, and it never would have occurred to the young man to carry a flask to an evening party. He carried it travelling on a hunting trip, but not to social gatherings for his host provided him with whatever might be necessary, and it did not brand a girl as a prig or unsociable if she did not join in whatever conviviality was going on in the way of drinking, but prohibition seems to have changed that to a certain extent so that the average girl of today faces the problem of learning very young how much she can drink of such things as whiskey and gin and sticking to the proper quantity.

One of the things that we hoped for in prohibition was protection for the weak, and I regret to say that conditions brought about by prohibition require more strength of character than any conditions I remember in my youth. The greater freedom of manners makes for franker and freer relationships between young men and women today. Some people think this a pity. Undoubtedly some of the old mystery and (glamour) is gone from this relationship but perhaps on the whole it is not a bad thing that boys and girls know each other a little bit better nowadays.

In one essential, things are undoubtedly far easier for the girl of today than they were for the girl of my generation. There are more avenues open to her for education and more ways in which she can earn her living and have an interesting life.

For this reason I feel that the girl of today, if she has sympathetic and wise parents, has a better chance of meeting her problems successfully and making her life a valuable and interesting one than had the girl of thirty years ago.

APPENDIX D: IS A WOMAN'S PLACE IN THE HOME?

By Mrs. Franklin D. Roosevelt

As I am talking to you for several weeks to come on women of today, let us state certain facts, and then some friends of mine, Mrs. Genevieve Forbes Herrick of Chicago and Miss Martha Strayer, newspaper woman of Washington, D. C., are waiting to ask me what they consider pertinent questions on these facts.

First, many people think this has already become a woman's world. I am quite willing to acknowledge that in certain ways women are rapidly wiping out the age-old superiority of the male, but I cannot say that I think we have yet reached the Amazon stage! It is still easier for men to do certain things than it is for women.

This advance in woman's position, of course, varies in different parts of the world, but it is clearly manifest everywhere. What we are primarily interested in is the way it is changing in our own country.

Man in his retreat is still using as his last ditch the old slogan of "woman's place is in the home," witness certain European countries, and a speaker before an educational meeting the other day who made this same proposal for the United States of America.

QUESTION: Do you think, Mrs. Roosevelt, that women's place is in the home?

ANSWER: That is an interesting question, Mrs. Herrick. Not long ago I saw a number of editorials saying that it was all very well for women to think that the work which they do outside of their homes is useful or important, but it is really negligible in comparison to the job of rearing a family. All women, however, are not born housekeepers, nurses, teachers, but no one will deny that the normal woman feels that her home must come first and that if she falls in love and can marry and have children, this is the life which will probably bring her the greatest lasting happiness.

Q. But how about the woman who does not fall in love and has to earn her own living?

A. Well, Miss Strayer, it seems to me that this is a most important question, for I am constantly surprised by the number of women who not only have to earn their own living but have to support dependents. Sometimes I think there are more mothers and younger brothers and sisters supported by their women relatives than by their men relatives. The boy of the family is apt to marry and have a family of his own. The girl feels the weight of her responsibility so much at home that even though she may fall in love, her responsibilities hold her and they even satisfy the inborn craving for a home and the ever present maternal instinct in every woman. The only sad part of it is that she must sometime find herself left alone. I see you smiling, Mrs. Herrick, and I realize, of course, that this may happen to married women.

Q. But, Mrs. Roosevelt, does that not seem to suggest that it would be well for the married woman to keep up some outside interests?

A. Personally, Mrs. Herrick, I believe that it (does). There is always an obligation among women to do church work and charitable work. The modern woman is beginning to realize that civic work and an interest in her government is almost more important than charitable work, because it strikes more fundamentally at the root of things which charity would alleviate but not exterminate, and now she has the vote, which places direct responsibility on her.

Q. Do you think, Mrs. Roosevelt, that women can be as good executives as men?

A. Yes, Miss Strayer. There is no question in my mind that such women who have ventured from the fireside have become increasingly important factors from the economic standpoint. They are achieving great success as producers and sellers of merchandise, and whether they are actively engaged in production or not, their taste and desires are the major consideration in many lines of business production. Women are at the head of large department stores, they are at the head of advertising agencies, they are editors of magazines. There is really no field of business (or) the professions where you cannot find a woman who has climbed to the top. This must mean that they are efficient executives. One interesting thing is that the "career" woman is not always the mannish woman as you might suppose, but frequently what is known as the extremely feminine type.

Q. Mrs. Roosevelt, it is always said that women are not successful in the creative arts. What do you think?

A. That has been true, Mrs. Herrick, but as a matter of fact, of late years women have been the greatest factor as patrons of the arts, and there are a few of them who have shown creative ability. In the fields of literature and...drama, I should say there are many women who stand on a par with the men. In other fields, however, they have not yet made such strides. Here and there you find the names of great women painters or sculptors or musicians, but this slower development may be because of the restrictions cast around the lives of women in the past, which have curtailed their freedom. Freedom is necessary for the development of the creative spirit which cannot be bound by the conventions. We cannot deny that for many years women have been hedged in by conventions to a far greater extent than have men. Yes, Miss Strayer.

Q. What would you say about women in the field(s) of religion and education?

A. I should say that in the field of religion, we do not claim many great women preachers. Women are supposed to be the talkers of the world, and yet the orators, both lay and ecclesiastic, seem to be primarily men. When it comes to ministering to the needs of humanity, to "taking care of the lost sheep," the women are (predominant) in the field of social service, and many stand preeminent.

Both men and women have been great educators. The business of education appeals to the maternal and the paternal instincts, and the honors in this field are almost equally divided. In the actual teaching profession, I think men and women are almost equally successful.

Q. Well, Mrs. Roosevelt, one last question. What do you think about women in the field of politics and public affairs?

A. (The) time was when only such women as could be counted on to do as they were told were allowed to hold party offices, but that day is over and done with. If a woman does as good work in politics as in other fields and chooses to be independent today, she is increasingly recognized and given a free hand to work out her own salvation just as the men do. She may have a few extra hurdles to jump, but nothing insurmountable will be put in her way. We are nearing a point, not when the world will be a woman's world, but where there shall be real equality between men and women.

I should say that the woman's place is in the home, but today her home is no longer (encompassed) by four walls nor her activities limited. This will be a great benefit to the human race, I believe. Biologically woman is the mother of the race. Through her the stream of life goes on.

A woman must have her own life just as a man has always had. She must live her own life. She cannot live her husband's nor her children's lives any more than they can or should live hers. She will undoubtedly become more efficient in developing this art of living, and this world, where men and women shall have equal opportunities and equal responsibilities, even though they may be different each from the other, may prove to be a more agreeable world for all of us to live in than the old one we are leaving behind.

APPENDIX E: FDR'S ACCEPTANCE TO RUN FOR FOURTH TERM

July 10, 1944

The president has received the following letter from Honorable Robert E. Hannegan, chairman, Democratic National Committee.

(Quotation marks at the beginning of each paragraph have been removed.)

Dear Mr. President:

As chairman of the Democratic National Committee, it is my duty on behalf of the committee to present for its consideration a temporary roll of the delegates for the national convention, which will convene in Chicago on July 19, 1944.

The national committee has received from the state officials of the Democratic Party certification of the action of the state conventions, and the primaries in those states which select delegates in that manner.

Based upon these official certifications to the national committee, I desire to report to you that more than a clear majority of the delegates to the national convention are legally bound by the action of their constituents to cast their ballots for your nomination as president of the United States. This action in the several states is a reflection of the wishes of the vast majority of the American people that you continue as president in this crucial period in the nation's history.

I feel, therefore, Mr. President, that it is my duty as chairman of the Democratic National Committee to report to you the fact that the national convention will during its deliberations in Chicago tender to you the nomination of the party as it is the solemn belief of the rank and file of Democrats, as well as many other Americans, that the nation and the world need the continuation of your leadership.

In view of the foregoing, I would respectfully request that you send to the convention or otherwise convey to the people of the United States and expression that you will again respond to the call of the party and the people. I am confident that the people recognize the tremendous burdens of your office, but I am equally confident that they are determined that you must continue until the war is won and a firm basis for abiding peace among men is established.

Respectfully,

Robert E. Hannegan

In reply, the president wrote Mr. Hannegan as follows:

Dear Mr. Hannegan:

You have written me that in accordance with the records a majority of the delegates have been directed to vote for my renomination for the office of president, and I feel that I owe to you, in candor, a simple statement of my position.

If the convention should carry this out, and nominate me for the presidency, I shall accept. If the people elect me, I will serve.

Every one of our sons serving in this war has officers from whom he takes his orders.

Such officers have superior officers. The president is the commander-in-chief and he, too, has his superior officer—the people of the United States.

I would accept and serve, but I would not run in, the usual partisan, political sense. But if the people command me to continue in this office and in this war, I have as little right to withdraw as the soldier has to leave his post in the line.

At the same time, I think I have a right to say to you and to the delegates to the coming convention something which is personal—purely personal.

For myself, I do not want to run. By next spring, I shall have president and commander-in-chief of the Armed Forces for twelve years—three times elected by the people of this country under the American constitutional system.

From the personal point of view, I believe that our economic system is on a sounder, more human basis than it was at the time of my first inauguration.

It is perhaps unnecessary to say that I have thought only of the good of the American people. My principal objective, as you know, has been the protection of the rights and privileges and fortunes of what has been so well called the average of American citizens.

After many years of public service, therefore, my personal thoughts have turned to the day when I could return to civil life. All that is within me cries out to go back to my home on the Hudson River, to avoid public responsibilities, and to avoid also the publicity which in our democracy follows every step of the nation's chief executive.

Such would be my choice. But we of this generation chance to live in a day and hour when our nation has been attacked, and when its future existence and the future existence of our chosen method of government are at stake..

To win this war wholeheartedly, unequivocally and as quickly as we can is our task of the first importance. To win this war in such a way that there be no further world wars in the foreseeable future is our second objective. To provide occupations, and to provide a decent standard of living for our men in the Armed Forces after the war, and for all Americans, are the final objectives.

Therefore, reluctantly, but as a good soldier, I repeat that I will accept and serve in this office, if I am so ordered by the commander-in-chief of us all—the sovereign people of the United States.

Very sincerely yours,

Franklin D. Roosevelt

APPENDIX F: ADDRESS BY THE PRESIDENT NOVEMBER 2, 1944

I had hoped that during the early part of this week, I could have gone in person to some of the nearer Midwestern cities, such as Cleveland and Detroit, and I had hoped that I could visit some of my old friends in upstate New York.

However, on my return to Washington from Chicago, I find that I am not free to spare the time right now. Therefore, I am speaking to you from the White House.

I am disappointed about this—but, as I told the American people when I became president, I follow the principle of first things first; and this war comes first.

We have all been overjoyed by the news from the far Pacific, eight thousand miles away. Never before in all of history has it been possible successfully to conduct such massive operations with such long lines of supply and communication.

In the Pacific theatre, even while we are fighting a major war in Europe, our advance toward Japan is many months ahead of our own optimistic schedule.

But we must remember that any military operation conducted at such a distance is a hazardous undertaking. In any long advance, progress may be interrupted by checks or setbacks. However, ultimately our advance will stop only in Tokyo itself.

Our success has been the result of planning and organization and building; it has been the result of the hardest work and the hardest fighting of which our people are capable.

On the other side of the world, in Europe, the Allied forces under General Eisenhower are pounding the Germans with relentless force.

We do not expect to have a winter lull in Europe. We expect to keep striking—to keep the enemy on the move—to hit him again and again—to give him no rest—and to drive through to the final objective—Berlin.

In Italy, against the handicap of rugged mountain obstacles, and against bitter German resistance—the Allied armies are steadily moving forward, wearing down the German fighting strength in a slow, hard slugging match.

In winning this war there is just one sure way to guarantee the minimum of casualties—by seeing to it that, in every action, we have overwhelming material superiority.

We have already sent to Europe—just one of our many fronts—a force greater than the entire American expeditionary force of 1918. American troops now are fighting along a battle-line of three hundred miles in France and about a hundred miles in Italy.

Within ten weeks after the first landings in France last June, the Allies had landed on the Normandy beaches nearly two million men, more than two million tons of supplies, and nearly half a million vehicles.

Think of all that vast mass of material for one operation—think of the war factories and ships and planes and railroads and labor required to produce and deliver the right supplies to the right place at the right time.

Then think of the tasks that lie ahead of us—all the long, tough miles to Berlin—all the major landings yet to be made in the Pacific—and you will have a conception of the magnitude of the job that remains to be done. It is still a job requiring the all-out production efforts of all of our people here at home.

Delays in the performance of our job at home mean prolonging the war. They will mean an increase in the total price we must pay in the lives of our men.

All of our able commanders in the field know this. And so do our soldiers and sailors. And we at home must never forget it.

All Americans at home are concerned in this—the fulfillment of an obligation to our fighting men.

The women of America are most profoundly concerned.

Today, women are playing a far more direct, more personal part in the war than ever before.

First, and I think rightly first, are those women who have gone into the WACS and the WAVES and the Marines and the Coast Guard, the nursing services of the army and navy, the Red Cross—serving in all kinds of places, in and out of the United States—all of them performing functions which definitely relieve men for combat work.

Then there are the millions of women who have gone into war industries. They are greatly responsible for the fact that the munitions and supplies to our men at the front have gone through to them on time.

And, finally, the women who uncomplainingly have done the job of keeping the homes going—the homes with service flags in the window—service flags with blue stars or gold stars.

And we do not forget those women who have volunteered with the men in the difficult and important work of the nation boards all over the nation—doing the job of apportioning the necessities of life equitably among their neighbors—rich and poor.

Everyone who has made a sacrifice in this war—and that includes one hundred and thirty-five million Americans—is determined that this must not happen again—that the disastrous mistakes of the past shall not be repeated—that this nation shall be committed to play a leading part in a world organization which shall be strong and effective and enduring.

We have been told during this political campaign that unless the American people elect the Republican presidential choice, the Congress will not cooperate in the peace. This is a threat to build a party spite-fence between us and the peace.

I do not know who empowers these men to speak for the Congress in uttering such a threat.

Certainly the United States Senate and the House of Representatives showed no reluctance to agree with the foreign policy of this administration when, almost unanimously last year, they passed the Connally and Fulbright resolutions which pledged this nation to cooperate in a world organization for peace.

These are high and serious matters to those who know how greatly our victory in this war and our ability to establish a lasting peace depend on maintaining unshaken that understanding which must be the core of the United Nations.

It is heartening for me to have known and to have talked with the statesmen of the smaller nations as well as our larger Allies—

men like Benes of Czechoslovakia, Mikolajczyk of Poland, Nygaardswold of Norway—and leaders of democratic thought from Yugoslavia and Greece and Denmark and Belgium and the Netherlands—and, of course, the great leaders of our neighbor countries in this hemisphere.

I have spent many fruitful hours talking with men from the more remote nations, such as Turkey, Persia, Arabia, Abyssinia, Liberia, Siam and others—for all of them are part and parcel of this great family of nations. It is only through an understanding acquired by years of consultation, that one can get a viewpoint of their problems and their innate yearnings for freedom.

And all of them have this in common—that they yearn for peace and stability, and they look to America with hope and faith.

The world is rising from the agony of the past; the world is turning with hope to the future. It would be a sorry and cynical thing to betray this hope for the sake of mere political advantage, and a tragic thing to shatter it because of the failure of vision.

There have been some other aspects of this campaign which have been distasteful to all of us.

This campaign has been marred by even more than the usual crop of whisperings and rumoring. Some of these get into print, in certain types of newspapers; others are traded about, secretly, in one black market after another. I do not propose to answer in kind.

The voting record proves that the American people pay little attention to whispering campaigns. They have paid little attention to all the malignant rumors of enemy origin which have flooded this country during this war—and I am sure they will treat the present whispering with the same contempt.

As we approach Election Day, more wicked charges may be made with the hope that someone or somebody will gain momentary advantage.

Hysterical, last minute accusations or sensational revelations are trumped up in an attempt to panic the people on Election Day.

But the American people are not panicked easily. Pearl Harbor proved that.

This election will not be decided on a basis of malignant murmurings—or shouts. It will be settled on the basis of the record.

We all know the record of our military achievements in this war.

And we all know the record of the tremendous achievements of our American farmers, our American business men, and our American labor.

And we all know the record of our teamwork with our Allies. Immediately after Pearl Harbor we formed with the other United Nations the greatest military coalition in world history. And we have steadily gone on from that to establish the basis for a strong and durable organization for world peace.

The America which built the greatest war machine in all history, and which kept it supplied, is an America which can look to the future with confidence and faith.

I propose the continuance of the teamwork that we have demonstrated in this war.

By carrying out the plans we have made we can avoid a postwar depression—we can provide employment for our veterans and our war workers—we can achieve an orderly reconversion.

Above all, we can avoid another false boom like that which burst in 1929, and a dismal collapse like that of 1930 to 1933.

With continuance of our teamwork, I look forward, under the leadership of this government, to an era of expansion and production and employment—to new industries and increased security.

I look forward to millions of new homes, fit for decent living; to new, low-priced automobiles; new highways; new airplanes and airports; to television; and miraculous, new inventions and discoveries, made during this war, which will be adapted to the peace-time uses of a peace-loving people.

The record that we have established in this war is one of which every American has a right to be proud—today and for all time.

We do not want the later record to say that the great job was done in vain.

We do not want our boys to come back to an America which is headed for another war in another generation.

Our post war job will be to work and to build—for a better America than we have ever known.

If in the next few years we can start that job right, then you and I will know that we have kept faith with our boys—we have helped them to win a total victory.

GRANDPA FOX
Probably about 1880-85

GRANDPA BRISTER - Probably
about 1885.

, March 17, 1968

ldren

Our father, the soldier 1913. He
was reported to be the healthiest
in his division. The doctors stopped
giving him shots. They said it was a
waste because none of themn took effect.

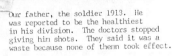

Mother, Daddy and all the
grandchildren that were in
existance in 1968

ME -Age about 4. Standing on the
running board of daddy's new
car (I think it was an Essick).
The occasion: Everyone gathered in
Big Lake, TX. to witness the blow in
of the first oil well.

Strange as it may seem, the big
handsome driller that decended from
the oil rig platform, drenched in
thick black oil, would become my
father-in-law some 30 years later.

COLONY SCHOOL - Depression kids 1934 or 5.
Teachers: Elsie Oliver Millican and
John Kirk Petty. The cute little boys with
long ties are Eugene and Rayfird Brister.
A.J and I are on back row.

Smokey Towerton, our best friend through the years.
He was about 16 when we moved to the Colony. He
went to work for daddy, helped build fence, sheared
sheep and goats and did whatever else. He was with
daddy the day the rattlesnake bit me.

He was a great story teller and could spin a yarn
about almost anything. He could yodel to rival the
singers in the Swiss Alps and could be heard for
miles when he was back in the hills.

The eight Brister brothers
1945. They are in line in o[
of age: A.J., Eugene, Rafor
Roy David, Emerson, Jack,
Vernon and Dewayne

There were always extra boys
around to play. This was
Eugene, Leonard Chambliss, Roy
David, Billy White, Raford,
Jack and Evelyn

A WAGON FULL OF BRISTER KIDS

A beautiful rock mountain that forms the bend in the creek that leads into the valley called home. Here another rock mountain takes over on the opposite side and creates Rough Creeks crooked path into scenic beauty that was no doubt what held facination for the young rancher seeking a home 82 years ago (1927). It is now a favorite camp site for the large family that originated here as they gather for family events

Mother and Daddy, March 17, 1968

All ten children

George and Jessie Brister on their
50th wedding anniversary,

50th anniversary - family grown to this.
No losses to death.

THE NEW YORK TIMES, THURSDAY, APRIL 8,

PRESIDENT MAKES FIRST SALE IN SECOND WAR LOAN DRIVE

The First War Bond Sale. The two girls in line worked in the office with me. I was next in line, but missed getting in photo. The cover page of a South American magazine did catch my face, but I do not know what has happened to my copy of that magazine

Fala, the President's much loved little Scotty was much in the spot light on this day. He sought my attention.

Fala
Pres Roosevelt's Scotty

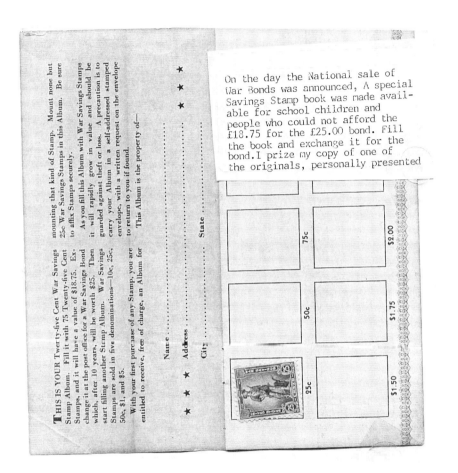

THIS IS YOUR Twenty-five Cent War Savings Stamp Album. Fill it with 75 Twenty-five Cent Stamps, and it will have a value of $18.75. Exchange it at the post office for a War Savings Bond which, after 10 years, will be worth $25. Then start filling another Stamp Album. War Savings Stamps are sold in five denominations—10c, 25c, 50c, $1, and $5.

With your first purchase of any Stamp, you are entitled to receive, free of charge, an Album for mounting that kind of Stamp. Mount none but 25c War Savings Stamps in this Album. Be sure to affix Stamps securely.

As you fill this Album with War Savings Stamps it will rapidly grow in value and should be guarded against theft or loss. A precaution is to carry your Album in a self-addressed stamped envelope, with a written request on the envelope to return to you if found.

This Album is the property of—

Name ....

Address ....

City .... State ....

On the day the National sale of War Bonds was announced, A special Savings Stamp book was made available for school children and people who could not afford the £18.75 for the £25.00 bond. Fill the book and exchange it for the bond. I prize my copy of one of the originals, personally presented

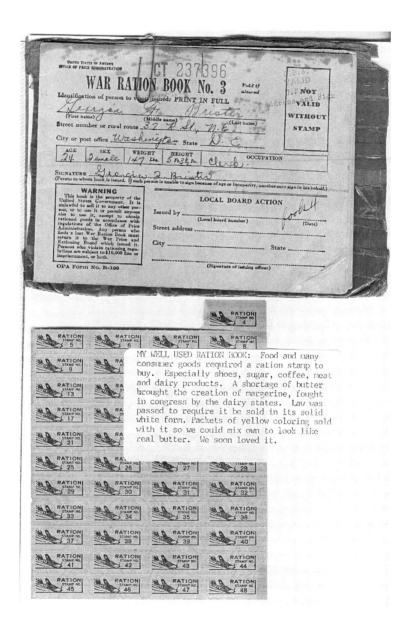

MY WELL USED RATION BOOK: Food and many consumer goods required a ration stamp to buy. Especially shoes, sugar, coffee, meat and dairy products. A shortage of butter brought the creation of margerine, fought in congress by the dairy states. Law was passed to require it be sold in its solid white form. Packets of yellow coloring sold with it so we could mix own to look like real butter. We soon loved it.

THE WHITE HOUSE

WASHINGTON

An interesting side light to the White House shows that the public does not change very much in its ways of thinking about any new advancement in civilization or ways of thinking.

In 1857 when the first bath tub was installed the criticism poured in just as badly as it does on any modern day suggested improvement. The criticism was that it was introducing an old Roman luxry into a Democracy where it had no place. Boston, Mass. even passed a law forbidding citizens to take a bath from early fall until late spring as a move against the use of bathtubs in America.

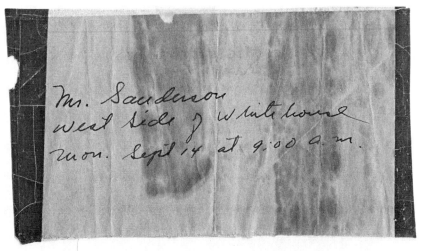

Mr. Sanderson
west side of White house
Mon. Sept 14 at 9:00 a.m.

1942 things were handled rather
informally. This is the original
note handed to me following the
three days of interrogation,
informing me that I had been
chosen for this special assignment.

My 24th birthday. My three
apartment mates and two co-workers

With the daily avalance of daily mail there were letters of the lighter nature.
This one addressed to Mr. Rubber Amistrator was received at the War Production
Board and passed on to Mrs. Roosevelt. Though sad, it does reveal the pain of
the shortage of consumer goods. It also reveals the need for all those expert
typists government girls. Copy machines were still in our future. Documents to
be shared had to be copied.

WAR PRODUCTION BOARD

WASHINGTON, D. C.

5001 New Municipal
Center Building

Dear Mr. President's Wife:

      Enclosed is a photostatic copy of a letter which I re-
ceived the other day. I think it is only fair that it should come
to your cognizance.

      If you put yourself in the position of the Rubber Di-
rector who, because of your husband's Directive, has to assume the
responsibility of answering this communication, I think that you
will realize the weighty burdens that are upon him.

      Very sincerely yours,

      /s/ Bradley Dewey
      Rubber Director

Santa Cruz, Calif.
Jan. 25, 1944
106 Mission St.

Dear Mr. rubber amistrator,

      When are you going to give us that elastix
you promised. My panties feall down to day at school,
and all the kids lauffed. I betcha Mr. Rosevelts panties
don't fall down, 'cause she is our president's wife and I
betcha you give her all the lastix she wants.

      Truly
        Yours

          Diane
          Lucille
          Berntzen

ARTICLE FROM SAN SABA NEWS

San Saba Girl Has Yule Visit With "F.D.R." and Wife

Here are excerpts from a letter written to her parents and family, the G. H. Bristers, by Miss Francis Brister, Washington, D. C., who is one of the secretaries in the office of Mrs. Franklin D. Roosevelt, wife of the president of the United States:

"I think it was very sweet of little Dwayne not to mind old Santa giving the toys to Uncle Sam. I noticed that too. Old Santa didn't have any toys for the little up here either.

"Last week was very busy for us...I really did enjoy this Christmas more than any since I have been away from home. In the first place, last Thursday we went to the President's office. Gee! It was a thrill to see the president. He looked so much better than he did the last time I saw him. He shook hands with each one of us and the way he would look at each of us and say, 'Merry Christmas, and I'm so glad to see you,' made each of us feel that no one else was in the room.

"Mrs. Roosevelt was standing behind his chair, but as charming a person as she is, I can hardly see her when he is to be seen at the same time. (I have been telling the girls that I never expect a greater man to hold my hand.) They gave us their card for 1943 and a crystal paper weight, with 'Christmas 1943 from F.D.R.' engraved on it.

"We have had awfully cold weather here all along, but in spite of the freezing temperature I went to midnight church services at the Washington Cathedral Christmas Eve. It was the first time I had ever been inside the Cathedral. It is truly the most magnificent church I have ever seen the inside of, and I never hope to see so many people in one church. The services were beautiful—I shall never forget them."

AUTOGRAPHED PHOTOGRAPH

Received day Mrs. Roosevelt
departed The White House

Eleanor Roosevelt wrote:

Many people will walk in and out of your life,
But only true friends will leave footprints in your heart.
To handle yourself, use your head;
To handle others, use you heart.
Anger is only one letter short of danger.
If someone betrays you once, it is his fault;
If he betrays you twice, it is your fault.
Great minds discuss ideas;
Average minds discuss events;
Small minds discuss people.
He who loses money, loses much;
He, who loses a friend, loses much more;
He, who loses faith, loses all.
Beautiful young people are accidents of nature,
But beautiful old people are works of art.
Learn from the mistakes of others.
You can't live long enough to make them all yourself.
Friends, you and me . . . You brought another friend . . .
And then there were . . . 3
We started our group . . . Our circle of friends . . .
And like that circle . . . There is no beginning or end . . .

Yesterday is history.
Tomorrow is mystery.
Today is a gift.

Energy to Burn
Vim of Guest Roosevelt Dazes English
By Gladwin Hill
Associated Press staff writer

London, Oct. 28—Englishmen are incredulous over "the eternal stimulus of the woman."

Mrs. Roosevelt has had that effect on them since her arrival at Britain five days ago.

The personal charm of America's First Lady has evoked pleased exclamations everywhere, but it is her tireless activity and the effortless way in which she spends whole days wearing out shoe-leather visiting was establishments that has caused them to top their hats in admiration.

In less than a week Mrs. Roosevelt has covered perhaps as much as a thousand miles just on jaunts around London. She has been on the go from as early as 7 a. m. to as late as 2 a. m. and has appeared in half a dozen different places in a day.

All the men in England were at war. The women took over the operation of the home front. In this picture, Mrs. Roosevelt (on the tractor) is making an inspection of the English farm women. The news clipping was from this trip. Note that her shoes wore out and she patched the holes with paper. Like the rest of us, Mrs. Roosevelt abided by the shoe rationing and would not ask for or accept special privileges.

THE WHITE HOUSE
WASHINGTON

Mrs. Roosevelt

requests the pleasure of the company of

Miss Brister

at a

Buffet Supper

Wednesday evening, January 31, 1945

at seven o'clock

Mrs. Roosevelt

At Home

on Friday afternoon

January 7, 1944

at five o'clock

Miss Georgia F. Brister

The honor of your presence

is requested at the ceremonies

attending the Inauguration of the

President of the United States

January twentieth,

Nineteen hundred forty-five.

Harry Flood Byrd, Chairman,

Kenneth McKellar, Arthur Vandenberg, Sam Rayburn,

Robert L. Doughton, Joseph W. Martin, Jr.

Committee on Arrangements.

Edwin A. Halsey, Secretary.

Please present the enclosed

Card of admission.

My invitation and pass to the inauguration
of President Roosevelt January 20, 1945.
Because of the war and the presidents
health, the usual pagentry of inauguration
not observed. The ceremony held on the
South Portico of The White House.
Invited guests stood in a deep snow on
the White House grounds, but the excitement
of the day kept us warm and protective
footware kept our feet dry and warm.

Miss Georgia F. Brister

WHITE HOUSE STAFF

Inauguration Ceremonies

JANUARY TWENTIETH, 1945

11:45 A. M.

ADMIT BEARER TO SECTION **B** OF THE WHITE HOUSE GROUNDS, LOCATED SOUTH OF THE PORTICO. ENTER SOUTHWEST GATE.

Harry F. Byrd

Chairman
Committee on Arrangements

NONTRANSFERABLE

A couple of special invitations

A party on January 7, 1944
A Buffet Supper with Mrs. Roosevelt
on January 31, 1945. Our
cancelled passes were returned
as souveniers of the occasions.

EAST ENTRANCE

Miss Georgia F Brister
will please present this card at
The White House
January 7, 1944
at 5 o'clock

NOT TRANSFERABLE

A sad day for the nation.
President Roosevelt's
body being returned to
The White House.

The flag-draped coffin bearing the body of President Roosevelt is borne into the White House, followed by Mrs. Roosevelt (right). She is escorted by Vice Admiral Wilson Brown, who was naval aide to President Roosevelt (extreme right), and White House Usher Charles Claunch (at Mrs. Roosevelt's left).

President Roosevelt's body lies in state in the east room of the White House with representatives of the armed forces standing guard beside the flower-banked casket. Simple funeral rites of the Episcopal Church were to be held at 4 p.m. today.
—Associated Press Photo.

1942
WITH
CHRISTMAS GREETINGS
AND OUR BEST WISHES
FOR A
HAPPIER NEW YEAR
THE PRESIDENT
AND
MRS. ROOSEVELT

1943
WITH CHRISTMAS GREETINGS
AND OUR BEST WISHES FOR A
HAPPIER NEW YEAR
THE PRESIDENT AND MRS. ROOSEVELT

With Christmas Greetings
and our best wishes
for a
Happier Nineteen Forty-five
The President
and
Mrs. Roosevelt

Christmas 1945

A Merry Christmas

from

The President and Mrs. Truman

CHRISTMAS CARDS 1942 - 1945 .

Always presented personally by the President
dring a reception for all employees

THE WHITE HOUSE
WASHINGTON

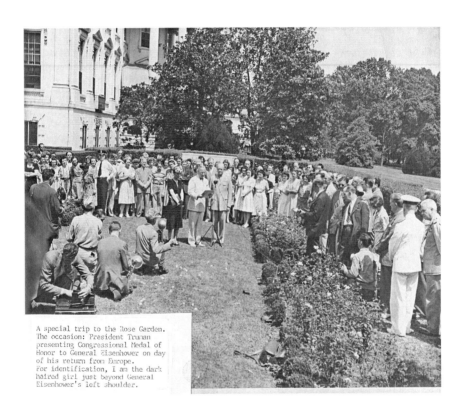

A special trip to the Rose Garden.
The occasion: President Truman
presenting Congressional Medal of
Honor to General Eisenhower on day
of his return from Europe.
For identification, I am the dark
haired girl just beyond General
Eisenhower's left shoulder.

President Truman and General
George C. Patton. Taken during
General Patton s last time home.
1945.

President Truman presenting the Medal of Distinguished Service to Press Secretary Steve Early. I am against the wall behind the President. Mr. Sanderson behind me to my left. Note size of the White House staff.

BIG HAIR days - 1971. Ready to
preside at Class banquet FUMC.

THE WHITE HOUSE

WASHINGTON

November 14, 1973

Dear Miss Morris:

I am deeply heartened by all the words of
encouragement which I am receiving at this
time -- and your message of support means
a great deal to me, especially since you
were a member of the White House Staff
yourself at one time. Your steadfastness
and confidence are truly heartening, and
they reaffirm my conviction that this Administration can continue to move toward
the great goals of peace, prosperity, and
social progress the American people
elected us to achieve.

With appreciation and best wishes,

Sincerely,

Richard Nixon

Miss Georgia B. Morris
6611 Pimlico
Dallas, Texas 75214

A letter received in
response to a note I
sent Pres. Nixon in the
dark days of Watergate